WRITERS
AND THEIR
NOTEBOOKS

WRITERS
AND THEIR
NOTEBOOKS

Edited by **DIANA M. RAAB**

The University of South Carolina Press

© 2010 University of South Carolina

Some of the material in this volume has appeared previously:

Reginald Gibbons, "My Own Particular Custom," © Reginald Gibbons, reprinted by permission, appeared in an earlier version in Sheila Bender, ed., *The Writer's Journal: 40 Contemporary Writers and Their Journals,* Delta, 1997.

Sue Grafton, "The Use of the Journal in Writing the Private Eye Novel," was previously published in *Writing the Private Eye Novel: A Handbook,* edited by Robert J. Randisi, published by Writers Digest Books in 1997, used with permission of the author.

Diana M. Raab, "Use Journaling to Spark Your Writing," first appeared in *The Writer* (October 2007).

Peter Selgin, "Keeping Up with the Days," was published in *Cincinnati Review* (Winter 2008).

Published by the University of South Carolina Press
Columbia, South Carolina 29208

www.sc.edu/uscpress

Manufactured in the United States of America

19 18 17 16 15 14 13 12 11 10   10 9 8 7 6 5 4 3 2 1

Library of Congress Cataloging-in-Publication Data

Writers and their notebooks / edited by Diana M. Raab.
     p. cm.
   Includes bibliographical references.
   ISBN 978-1-57003-865-5 (cloth : alk. paper) — ISBN 978-1-57003-866-2 (pbk. : alk. paper)
   1. Authors, American—20th century—Diaries. 2. Authors, American—20th century—Biography. 3. Authorship. I. Raab, Diana, 1954–
   PS129.W738 2010
   808'.06692—dc22

                                                              2009029723

This book was printed on Glatfelter Natures, a recycled paper with 30 percent

CONTENTS

FOREWORD

The tenth-century Japanese court lady Sei Shonagon kept a writer's note-book in which she recorded a miscellaneous catch-all of things charming and annoying, rhapsodic descriptions of nature, odd facts, and malicious observations of her countrymen. She claimed to be chagrined when it was discovered and read, though a part of her must, at least subconsciously, have had readers in mind all along. Now considered an indispensable classic, Shonagon's *The Pillow Book* was also, if you will, an early blog.

Writing is one way of self-making. That a would-be author often nur-tures to life a professional literary voice, as Sei Shonagon did, through the act of keeping a notebook, is a phenomenon to which many writers in this sparkling, splendidly useful anthology bear witness. These essayists find numerous ways to pay homage to their notebooks, which they describe metaphorically as: a laboratory, a mirror, a brainstorming tool, an icebreaker, a wailing wall, a junk drawer, a confessional, a postcard to oneself, singing in the shower, a playground for the mind, a jump-start cable, a memory aid, an archive, an anthology, a warehouse, a tourist's camera, a snooping device, a role-playing arena, an observation-sharpener, a survival kit, a way of documenting mental illness, a meditation practice, masturbation, a witness stand, a therapist, a housekeeper, a spiritual advi-sor, a compost bin, a punching bag, a sounding-board, a friend.

Such sweet-natured gratitude is expressed to these journals, as though their coming to be filled with words were an accident of grace performed by someone else, like a genie! The writer and the journal-keeper are some-times two, companionate, sometimes one, indivisible. Oh, there is the occasional resentful note, the fear of surrendering your life to the practice of journaling, of being lured into narcissism, hypergraphia, or gruesome addiction. And there are the lingering uncertainties: should the notebook be spiral or bound? A book or computer file? Written in every day or only when the mood strikes? Performed in private or in public, at home or at a library or cafe? Is a writer's journal a separate literary genre, to be parsed by scholars, or just a more pretentious diary? Should the prose be rough, untrammeled, uncensored, or artfully composed, like finger exercises for a pianist? Arguments can be made on either side; and, generally speaking, every side turns up in these pages.

I salute the editor of this valuable collection, Diana M. Raab, who has done such a sensitive job of gathering these diverse, eloquent, and experienced voices, and encouraging their thoughtful, heartbreaking, rambunctious, free flights of testimony and speculation into being. Freedom is a frequent theme in these pages. The freedom to try out things, to write clumsy sentences when no one is looking, to be unfair, immature, even to be stupid. No one can expect to write well who would not first take the risk of writing badly. The writer's notebook is a safe place for such experiments to be undertaken.

Above all, the writer's notebook is an invitation to the Muse. The phonic similarity between the words *muse* and *musing* seems suddenly to make perfect sense. We call to our better self (another name for Muse) with these intimate scribbles.

Phillip Lopate

PREFACE

As artists have sketchbooks, writers have notebooks. Whether they choose to call them notebooks, journals, or daybooks, their motives are the same—to capture and document thoughts, sentiments, observations, ideas, ruminations, and reflections before these vanish.

The notebook may be thought of as a parking spot for the writer's ideas. It's the writer's studio and workshop—a place to collect and make discoveries about language, passions, obsessions, and curiosities. It's a place to scribble. There is no formula for keeping a notebook. The concept is that it should contain free-writing and memory triggers that will serve as vehicles to inspire future work. The notebook is akin to the author's other brain, the brain that has the freedom to think and muse freely with total recall. Writer Francine du Plessix Gray says this about journaling: "Our emotions, and the power of their expression, are kept at a maximum by the daily routine of being inserted into the journal's sharpening edge." She says that keeping a journal is like sharpening a pencil.

For the most part, the words on the pages of a journal are the music and voice of one's true emotions. The pages of the journal make no judgments and should be free of editors, critics, and teachers. Whether the writer is expressing deeply held beliefs, recording snippets of overheard dialogue, making observations, listing ideas for future projects, or copying a favorite poem, the notebook should be a vital part of the creative tool kit.

The art of journal writing dates back to when our ancestors wrote on cave walls. The first published journals were those kept by Samuel Pepys in the seventeenth century. Between 1660 and 1669 he wrote an eleven-volume diary that was published after his death in 1825. The journals of the Lewis and Clark Expedition appeared in the late 1700s and early 1800s. Then came James Swan, a Native American, who wrote extensively about whaling practices in the mid-1800s.

Walt Whitman wrote in his journal in the mid-1860s, and Ralph Waldo Emerson wrote about activities and friends of special interest to him, including about the author and naturalist Henry David Thoreau. In 1885, when Susy Clemens, the daughter of Mark Twain, was thirteen years old, she began to write a memoir of her experiences with her celebrated father. Virginia Woolf, one of the twentieth century's most influential writers, said that she wrote in her diary to bring order to the chaos in her life.

Some private diaries, such as those of Woolf, John Cheever, André Gide, May Sarton, Anaïs Nin, and Anne Frank have become published literary masterpieces. A more comprehensive list may be found in "Sources and Further Readings."

My inspiration for creating this book originates from my own experience and the joy that journaling has brought into my own life. For more than forty years, journaling has helped ground me during good and bad times. When I was ten, my mother gave me my first journal to help me cope with the loss of my beloved grandmother. My mother's very thoughtful gesture resulted in a lifetime passion for writing and served as the foundation and platform for my writing career. Today my library has a shelf completely devoted to my completed journals, which can be found in every shape and color, with pages both lined and unlined.

My first journal still remains quite vivid in my mind. It was a maroon, hardcover volume with the prophet Kahlil Gibran's wise sayings inscribed at the top of each page. For months after losing my grandmother, I poured my grief onto its pages. As an only child of working parents, I saw my journal as my best friend and confidant. Initially my musings were a form of catharsis in an effort to ease the pain of losing my grandmother, but subsequent entries became a pastime and a way to document the sentiments inherent in growing up, including the angst associated with adolescence and young adulthood.

My first book, *Getting Pregnant and Staying Pregnant: Overcoming Infertility and High-Risk Pregnancy,* began as a journal of my bed rest experience. Eventually I condensed the journal into an introduction for a self-help book for women also dealing with difficult pregnancies. In fact, in 2009 the book was revised and updated under the new title *Your High Risk Pregnancy: A Practical and Supportive Guide.*

In 2001, when my children began university and just after the Trade Centers tumbled to the ground, I enrolled in the charter class of Spalding

University's M.F.A. in Writing program. While majoring in creative non-fiction, I read the four published volumes of Anaïs Nin's journals and became even more inspired to continue my journal-keeping practices. Nin's first journal entry began as a letter to her deranged father, who left the family when she was twelve. I was very drawn to her writing style and sensibilities, and these books are still perched on the shelves of my writing studio. I often return to her volumes when my own muse takes a well-deserved break. I have found that Nin's words awaken the Muse inside of me.

The essays in this collection are a celebration of writers who use their notebooks to inspire, record, and document anything and everything which may nurture or spark their creative energy. These writers represent a broad spectrum of genres, including poetry, fiction, and nonfiction. They are male, female, young, old, and live from coast to coast. All of these authors have been widely published, and many are professors at major colleges and universities.

The confessional nature of their essays makes each one compelling in its own right. Many authors in this collection write so automatically in their notebooks that they were honestly stumped when asked to write an essay describing their actual practice. After minimal contemplation, they agreed, and by the time they reached the end of writing their essays, nearly all of them experienced an enormous sense of satisfaction. In fact, many thanked me for the exercise and the opportunity to share their sentiments about journaling. Many admitted to have learned more about themselves and their writing practices.

The motives for keeping a notebook vary. Some of the contributors use their journals while concurrently working on a literary project while others store their completed notebooks away for future use. For example, mystery writer Sue Grafton uses her journal as a companion to her work-in-progress. Poet Kim Stafford uses his entries as seeds for future poems. To illustrate how their notebooks have been used in future works, some of the contributors have actually shared journal entries to show how they evolved into published works.

Writers and nonwriters alike who have made journaling a vibrant part of their lives will agree to its benefits. The writers in this collection all concur in regard to the huge rewards of keeping a notebook. Even if life has gotten in the way of their own regular record-keeping, they advocate the practice to their students and colleagues.

This collection offers an extraordinary diversity of perspectives held together by one common thread—all contributors have a deep passion for keeping a notebook. Some choose to use it as a tool for survival or travel, some see it as a muse, and for others it's simply a habit that they have carried with them since childhood.

I now invite you, the reader, to take a peek inside the heads of these writers and what drives them—not only to the blank manuscript page, but also to the pages of their notebooks. It is my hope that their voices will inspire you to follow suit.

ACKNOWLEDGMENTS

I am grateful to all the wonderful contributors in this collection who have expressed utmost enthusiasm on writing an essay about their notebook-keeping practices. They have been a fabulous group to work with and I applaud all of their efforts.

I would also like to thank Carol Givner and Maggie Lang for their conscientious editorial support and Linda Fogle, Curtis Clark, Bill Adams, and the University of South Carolina Press for believing in this project from the beginning and for their help in bringing it to fruition. Special thanks go to David Starkey, Marcia Meier, Jean Harfenist, Susan Chiavelli, and Susan Gulbranson for their interest in this project and for their friendships.

As always, I am grateful to my family: my mother, Eva Marquise, for buying me my first journal; my husband, Simon; and our children, Rachel, Regine, and Joshua, who've supported all of my literary endeavors. I am in awe of your love.

Part 1

THE JOURNAL AS TOOL

A writer uses a journal to try out the new step in front of the mirror.

Mary Gordon, "The Country Husband,"
New York Times, October 6, 1991

JOURNALING—
A STEPPING STONE

James Brown

For me the journal is a tool—a stepping stone to a larger, more refined work that could be a memoir, a novel, a short story, the personal essay, or a script.

I don't keep a journal for the sake of recording random thoughts or feelings or simply the day's events, as you might in a diary, though I don't for a second discount the value of others doing so. The sheer act of writing, regardless of the form or its aim, is in and of itself a worthwhile endeavor.

I believe you discover what it is you want to say during the writing process. In fact, what you originally thought you wanted to say, and what you actually end up writing, aren't always the same things. I used to think that it was a shortcoming, not being able to stick with what I initially imagined myself writing, but now I see it as a strength.

I'm capable of changing for the better. I'm able to recognize previously unforeseen opportunities and capitalize on them. The work is malleable—an evolving, living thing in a constant state of flux. Getting to the good stuff is sometimes a process of elimination of the bad stuff in order to be able to see it for what it is. Then you discard it and take another shot—same material, same characters—only you do it from a different angle.

Maybe you hit pay dirt.

Maybe you sink again.

The point is you're at least one step closer to knowing what belongs in your story by knowing what does not.

The Irish writer Frank O'Connor reworked some of his stories seven or eight times even *after* they were published. That might seem a little obsessive, but then again I don't know any good writers who aren't. It seems to be the nature of the profession. Alcoholism runs a close second, and I occasionally wonder if it isn't because of all the frustration involved in finding the right story and telling it well.

This is where journaling comes in handy.

It can be a simple act of brainstorming, no boundaries or constraints. Fifties Beat writer Jack Kerouac used to put a roll of butcher paper into his typewriter and go at it like a wild man, more or less just writing whatever came into his head. The difference here is that Kerouac sometimes considered this material finished work; he didn't always go back and revise, so some of his published writing is pretty messy and difficult to read. It did not help matters that he was also frequently under the influence of amphetamines, in particular, Benzedrine. In any case, brainstorming helps take the pressure off you, the kind of pressure that comes from trying to imagine too much of your story at once, the kind of pressure that makes you freeze up and give up.

By journaling without constraint, writer's block ceases to exist. Even if it turns out you can't use much or anything you've written in your current work, it's gotten you writing. It's helped loosen you up.

Though I don't consider myself a screenwriter, I've written several screenplays based on novels of mine that were optioned for movies, and once I wrote a TV script for *21 Jump Street,* an old cop show. This was back in the early nineties, ancient history but still timely in terms of the subject and how I used journaling techniques to help me put the script together. I was a freelancer who lucked into the job on a producer friend's recommendation.

What he basically did, besides get me there, was give me the premise of a story: A teenager fresh out of juvie for stealing cars and hawking the parts, what's called "chopping," returns to his old neighborhood where he attempts to go straight instead of succumbing to his old criminal ways.

It's your standard good versus evil setup. Temptation is around every corner, and it was up to me, as the writer, to come up with the different characters and scenarios that best showed the boy struggling to do the right thing.

For me it's all about character. You can have the best plot in the world, but if the characters are stiff, clichéd, and one-dimensional, the story falls apart. If no one cares about the people in your story, certainly no one will care about what happens to them; if they don't care about what happens to them, it means they can't possibly care about the plot. The two elements are inescapably intertwined. Story, or plot, is a natural outgrowth of character. And because character defines action and action defines character (I'd like to take credit for this, but Aristotle said it first.), the brainstorming for me begins with character.

So who is this kid who steals cars and parts them out? What's his background? Where does he live? How does he live? How does he dress? What're his weaknesses? His strengths? What, in short, makes him tick?

In my journal, before I began the script, I tried to get a stronger conception of my central character by writing a short biography. The show originally aired in 1991 under the title "Second Chances," the last episode ever filmed of *21 Jump Street,* and to write the piece for this collection, it took an hour or more of sifting through dusty boxes in a dusty attic to find my old notes. They're nearly twenty years old, the ink has faded, and in a few spots I can't even make out the writing anymore. Those parts I omit with ellipses, and forgive the punctuation, or lack thereof, as I often throw the rules of grammar to the wind when I'm journaling:

> His name is Nick Capelli, he's of Irish and Italian descent, and his father bailed on him when he was twelve and most needed the guidance. . . . At heart he's good kid, but he's scared, too, given the rough neighborhoods he's lived in, and so he tries to act tough . . . walks with a swagger. Carries a knife and sometimes likes to pull it out in front of the mirror in his bedroom like DeNiro in Taxi Driver. His mom has a drinking problem, but she's not to blame for him screwing up, and it hurts her every time he does, but she has no real power over him anymore . . . he wants to go straight because he feels he's letting his mom down, but he's good at stealing cars, and like any kid he takes pride in his talents even if those talents are used illegally. There's a very pretty, shy girl in school he has crush on, and she'd like to get to know him better, but his reputation precedes him, and her parents won't let her date him. . . . He's shy, too. This could be another story line. Think about it.

The biography continues for another page, but this excerpt is enough to get a sense of how I used the journal to help me learn about the main character I wanted to create. Not everything I wrote found a place in the script—that wasn't the intention of the sketch—but one scene and an actual storyline did come from it. For the scene, I show Nick coming home from work and finding his mother drunk and in bed with her boyfriend, and if I remember correctly, to get him out of the apartment, she sends him to the store for a pack of cigarettes. The storyline involves the girl Nick likes and ultimately leads to the writing of several different scenes dramatizing their situation and the forces that keep them apart. In the end, however, the relationship angle took up too much screen time and was dropped for a less complicated version.

But that's another story.

What matters is how journaling can help the writer come up with ideas, kind of a warm-up to a bigger process. The next step is building on those ideas, discarding some and fleshing out others, developing characters and motives, and arranging the scenes in a logical, meaningful sequence with a firm sense of a beginning, middle, and end. Whether you write your thoughts down in a journal or try to store them all in your head, which I don't recommend, story begins when you begin to dream and brainstorm about people and their problems. Heroes without flaws, like stories without tension, offer little insight into the human condition.

We learn more from our losses and mistakes than our successes and victories. Better the protagonist changes and grows as a result of his or her trials and tribulations than languishes in ignorance, no wiser for the journey. In my own life I've made plenty of mistakes, too many, but I like to think I haven't repeated them all. Regret and guilt are sometimes our wisest companions. Keeping a journal, if you're capable of being honest with yourself, can facilitate a deeper understanding of the role you've played in some of life's conflicts. The same is true for storytelling. Our characters either overcome their troubles or succumb to them, and inherent in the term *succumb* is defeat. Those who give up against adversity or fail to learn from their personal blunders don't garner our respect, and after a while, if they don't take responsibility for themselves, they lose our interest and empathy.

I've written a few novels, a collection of short stories, and most recently a memoir titled *The Los Angeles Diaries*. The jacket copy describes it as follows: "Plagued by the suicides of both his siblings, heir to alcohol and drug abuse, divorce and economic ruin, James Brown lived a life clouded by addiction, broken promises and despair. . . . Personal failure, heartbreak, the trials for writing for Hollywood and the life-shattering events finally convince Brown that he must 'change or die.'"

It's a cheery little book, just two hundred pages, but it took me four years to write and thirty-plus to gather the materials to write it. Going in, before I even began taking notes, I had some definite ideas about how I wanted to structure the book. I'd read too many autobiographies and memoirs that paid close attention to chronology, too close in my opinion, and it came at a cost. Often the connecting material linking one event to another simply to maintain a linear structure struck me as expendable.

Not all experience is worth chronicling.

Maybe something significant happened to you as a junior in high school. Maybe that's when you suffered your first heartbreak. If you were to follow a tight chronology you might feel obliged to begin the story in your freshman year when you first laid eyes on the person who would later break your heart and work forward from there. The next thing you know, in order to get from point A to point B, you're filling pages with extraneous details just to pass the time, so you can get to your main story. That's what I wanted to avoid in *The Los Angeles Diaries*. The fluff. The filler.

The events that serve most to shape and define us are often the most tragic and blessed ones. That's what I was after in my memoir. I wanted to isolate the most defining moments in life and construct stories around them. The suicide of my brother. The suicide of my sister. Our mother's arrest. And since memory itself is by no means sequential, I decided to skip around in time. In one chapter I'm forty-something, in the next I'm six, but in the end I've covered the central periods of life. Childhood. Adolescence. Middle age. There's a beginning, middle, and end—just not in that order.

So how does this relate to journaling?

Where for the script I used the journal to write a character biography, in the case of the memoir I recorded specific memories. A pivotal moment in the lives of my brother, sister, and me was when sheriff's deputies came to arrest our mother on suspicion of murder and arson. I wrote these notes mostly to help me recall the details of that ugly night, and I used them not just in the memoir but also in an earlier book, *Final Performance*, an autobiographical novel revolving around many of the same subjects and events I deal with in *The Los Angeles Diaries*:

Remember the night they came for Mom. Remember you and Barry and Marilyn stretched out on the floor. We're watching TV. What was playing? The Blob? House of Wax? I'm not sure, but I know it was a scary movie. Mom either heard them first or saw them first or both. The tick of gravel beneath the tires of the cruiser coming into the driveway, headlights off, motor dead. She grabbed us and pulled us behind the couch. I remember she was in her nightgown and she was scared. We were all scared. The smell of her sweat. Flashlights through the living room windows, the beams crisscrossing on the ceiling. She holds you tight.

The compilation of one authentic detail after another makes for vivid, memorable prose. This particular entry recalls visceral details of smell, sight, and touch, and I later basically just lifted what I'd written in the journal and constructed a scene from it. Of course, it all needed lots of work, but from that scene I built a story.

The journal is a tool, and I've used it to write character biographies before beginning a story, while I'm actually writing the story, and sometimes even afterward when I have a first draft done but don't feel I've fully captured my characters. In my college creative writing classes I occasionally require the students to keep a journal and use it to sketch scenes and create fictional biographies for the stories they plan to write. Sometimes I ask them to go to the local Starbucks and eavesdrop on a conversation, recording it verbatim, so that they can see the difference between real talk and the polished dialogue in the books I have them read.

As a writer of highly personal fiction and nonfiction, I extract from my journals the fragments of memory and shoot to make them whole. In that process more details inevitably reveal themselves and further enrich the work. Memory is fallible, however. The powers of recollection fade with age; mental images, sensory details, old feelings, and emotions are all too often driven beneath the surface of our consciousness. This is especially true of memories that are painful to recall, and for some maybe that's a good thing, because in forgetting there may follow a necessary peace. Writers, however, can't afford the same luxury. We need to hang on to our experiences, both the crushing and joyous, and through reflection, either by keeping a journal before we begin a project or during its writing, we hope to come to a better understanding of who we are, what we've become, and where we're going. That's where you'll find your best stories, the ones that make sense out of the chaos we call our lives.

THE USE OF THE
JOURNAL IN WRITING
THE PRIVATE EYE NOVEL

Sue Grafton

The most valuable tool I employ in the writing of a private eye novel is the working journal. The process is one I began in rudimentary form when I first started work on *"A" Is for Alibi,* though all I retain of that journal now are a few fragmentary notes. With *"B" Is for Burglar,* I began to refine the method and from *"C" Is for Corpse* on, I've kept a daily log of work in progress. This notebook (usually four times longer than the novel itself) is like a letter to myself, detailing every idea that occurs to me as I proceed. Some ideas I incorporate, some I modify, many I discard. The journal is a record of my imagination at work, from the first spark of inspiration to the final manuscript. Here I record my worries and concerns, my dead ends, my occasional triumphs, all the difficulties I face as the narrative unfolds. The journal contains solutions to all the problems that arise in the course of the writing. Sometimes the breakthroughs are sudden; more often the answers are painstakingly arrived at through trial and error.

One of my theories about writing is that the process involves an ongoing interchange between Left Brain and Right. The journal provides a testing ground where the two can engage. Left Brain is analytical, linear, the timekeeper, the bean counter, the critic and editor, a valuable ally in the shaping of the mystery novel or any piece of writing for that matter. Right Brain is creative, spatial, playful, disorganized, dazzling, nonlinear, the source of the *Aha!* or imaginative leap. Without Right Brain, there would be no material for the Left Brain to refine. Without Left Brain, the jumbled brilliance of Right Brain would never coalesce into a satisfactory whole.

In addition to the yin/yang of the bicameral brain, the process of writing is a constant struggle between the Ego and the Shadow, to borrow Jungian terms. Ego, as implied, is the public aspect of our personality, the carefully constructed persona, or mask, we present to the world as the "truth" about us. The Shadow is our Unconscious, the Dark Side—the dangerous, largely unacknowledged cauldron of "unacceptable" feelings and reactions that we'd prefer not to look at in ourselves and certainly hope to keep hidden from others. We spend the bulk of our lives perfecting our public image, trying to deny or eradicate the perceived evil in our nature.

For the writer, however—especially the mystery writer—the Shadow is crucial. The Shadow gives us access to our repressed rage, the murderous impulses that propel antisocial behavior whether we're inclined to act out or not. Without ingress to our own Shadow, we would have no way to delineate the nature of a fictional killer, no way to penetrate and depict the inner life of the villain in the novels we write. As mystery writers, we probe this emotional black swamp again and again, dredging in the muck for plot and character. As repelled as we may be by the Dark Side of our nature, we're drawn to its power, recognizing that the Shadow contains enormous energy if we can tap into it. The journal is the writer's invitation to the Shadow, a means of beckoning to the Unconscious, enticing it to yield its potent magic to the creative process.

What Goes into the Journal and How Does It Work?

At the outset of each new novel, the thing I do is open a document on my word processor that I call "Notes" or "Notes-1." By the end of a book, I have four or five such documents, averaging fifty single-spaced pages apiece.

In my first act of the writing day, I log into my journal with the date. Usually I begin with a line about what's happening in my life. I make a note if I'm coming down with a cold, if my cat's run away, if I've got company coming in from out of town. Anything that specifically characterizes the day becomes part of the journal on the theory that exterior events have the potential to affect the day's work. If I have a bad day at work, I can sometimes track the problem to its source and try correcting it there. For instance, if I'm consistently distracted every time I'm scheduled for a speaking engagement, I can limit outside events until the book is done.

The second entry in the journal is a note about any idea that's occurred to me in the dead of night, when Shadow and Right Brain are most active. Often, I'm wakened by a nudge from Right Brain with some suggestion about where to go next in the narrative or offering a reminder of a beat I've missed. Sometimes, I'm awakened by emotion-filled dreams or the horror of a nightmare, either one of which can hold clues about the story I'm working on. It's my contention that our writing is a window to all of our internal attitudes and emotional states. If I sit down to write and I'm secretly worried about the progress I'm making, then that worry will infuse the very work itself. If I'm anxious about an upcoming scene, if I'm troubled by the pacing, if I suspect a plot is too convoluted, or the identity of the killer is too transparent, then the same anxiety will inhibit the flow of words. Until I own my worries, I run the risk of self-sabotage or writer's block. The journal serves as a place to offload anxiety, a verbal repair shop when my internal writing machine breaks down.

Generally, the next step in the journal is to lay out for myself where I am in the book. I talk to myself about the scene I'm working on, or the trouble spots as I see them. It's important to realize that the journal in progress is absolutely private—*for my eyes only.* This is not a literary *oeuvre* in which I preen and posture for some future biographer. This is a nuts-and-bolts format in which I think aloud, fret, whine and wring my hands. There's nothing grand about it and it's certainly not meant to be great writing. Once a novel is finished and out on the shelves, then the journal can be opened to public inspection if I so choose.

In the safety of the journal, I can play "Suppose . . ." and "What if . . ." creating an atmosphere of open debate where Ego and Shadow, Left Brain and Right, can all be heard. I write down all the story possibilities . . . all the pros and cons . . . and then check back a day or so later to see which prospects strike a chord. The journal is experimental. The journal functions as a playground for the mind, a haven where the imagination can cavort at will. While I'm working in the journal, I don't have to look good. I can be as dumb or goofy as I want. The journal provides a place where I can let my proverbial hair down and "dare to be stupid," as we used to say in Hollywood.

The beauty of the journal entry is that before I know it, I'm sliding right into my writing for the day. Instead of feeling resistant or hesitant, the journal provides a jump-start, a way to get the words moving.

To demonstrate the technique, I'll include a few sample pages from the journal I kept during the writing of *"G" Is for Gumshoe.* I do this without embarrassment (she said), though I warn you in advance that what you see is a fumbling process, my tortured mind at work.

"G" Is for Gumshoe is essentially a "road picture." In this seventh novel in the series, Kinsey Millhone discovers she's on Tyrone Patty's hit list, targeted for assassination in retaliation for her part in his arrest and conviction. The following passages of the journal begin some three chapters into the novel. Earlier notes, unfortunately, were lost to me in the transfer of the work from an old computer system to newly acquired equipment. My intention here is not to try to dazzle you with my song-and-dance work, but to demonstrate the mundane level at which the journal actually functions.

1–2–89

Just checking in to have a little chat. I'm in Chapter 3 and feeling pretty good, but I'm wondering if I don't need some tension or suspense. We know there may be a hit man after her. She's currently on her way to the desert and everything seems really normal . . . nay, even dull. Do I need to pep it up a bit? She's almost at the Slabs. I've been doing a lot of description but maybe I need to weave it into the narrative better. Flipping back and forth from the external to the internal.

What other possibilities are there? I've noticed that with Dick Francis, sometimes when nothing's happening, you sit there expecting something anyway. I could use the external as a metaphor for the internal. I know I'll be doing that when Dietz enters the scene. What could Kinsey be thinking about while she drives down to the Slabs? She's talked briefly. . . .

1–4–89

Can't remember what I meant to say in the paragraph above. I did some work last night that I'm really happy with. I'm using a little boy with a toy car at the rest stop. Added a father asleep on the bench. Later, he turns out to be one of the guys hired to kill her.

Want to remember to use a couple of things.

1. When the mother dies, Kinsey goes back down to the desert with Dietz. They search, finding nothing . . . maybe a few personal papers. What they come across, in an old cardboard box under the trailer, is some objects . . . maybe just old cups & saucers (which may trigger memories in Irene Gersh . . .). But the newspapers in which

these objects are packed dated back to 1937 . . . Santa Teresa. Obviously, the mother was there at some point.

When Kinsey checks into the mother's background, she realizes Irene's birth certificate is a total fake. The mother has whited-out the real information, typed over it, and has done a photocopy. All the information has been falsified. She's not who she says she was during her lifetime . . . father's name is wrong. . . . I was thinking it might be Santa Teresa, but then Irene would know at the outset she had some connection with the town. Better she should think she was born in Brawley or someplace like that.

Kinsey tries to track down the original in San Diego . . . or wherever I decide to place the original . . . no record of such a birth. Once Kinsey finds the old newspapers, she decides to try Santa Teresa records, using the certificate # which is the only thing that hasn't been tampered with. Up comes the true certificate.

Must remember that a social security card . . . first three digits indicate where the card was issued. That might be a clue.

Irene Gersh is floored. If mom isn't who she claims she was, then who am I?

Must also remember that mom is frightened to death. That would be a nice murder method.

In addition to storyboarding ideas, I use my journal to record notes for all the research I've done. I also make a note of any question that occurs to me while I'm writing a scene. Instead of stopping the flow of words, I simply jot down a memo to myself for later action.

Journals often contain the ideas for scenes, characters, plot twists, or clever lines of dialogue that don't actually make it into the book I'm working on. Such literary detritus might well provide the spark for the next book in the series.

Often, too, in the pages of a journal, I'll find Right Brain leaping ahead to a later scene in the book. Since I don't actually outline a novel in any format or detailed way, the journal is a road map to the story I'm working on. If dialogue or a descriptive passage suddenly occurs to me, I'll tuck it in the journal and come back to it when I reach the chapter where the excerpt belongs. This way, I find I can do some of my writing in advance of myself. Right Brain, my creative part, really isn't interested in working line-by-line. Right Brain sees the whole picture, like the illustration on the box that contains a jigsaw puzzle. Left Brain might insist that we start at the beginning and proceed in an orderly fashion right through to the end, but Right Brain has its own way of going about its business. The journal is a place to honor Right Brain's ingenuity and non-conformity.

Sometimes I use the journal to write a note directly to Shadow or Right Brain, usually when I'm feeling blocked or stuck. These notes are like writer's prayers and I'm always astonished at how quickly they're answered.

In the *"G" Is for Gumshoe* journal, you can see that by March, some three months later, the book has advanced almost magically. I'll do a hop-skip-and-jump, picking up entries here and there.

3–12–89

Finally got Dietz & Kinsey on the road. They've stopped for lunch. She's asking him about his background & he's being good about that stuff. Want to keep them moving . . . let information surface while they're heading for Santa Teresa. Don't want the story to come to a screeching halt while they chit chat. Must keep defining his character through action . . . not just dialogue. Once I get the book on body-guarding techniques, I can fill in some technical information that will make him seem very knowledgeable. For now, I can do the small touches. At some point, he should give her some rules & regulations.

What else do I want to accomplish on the way up to Santa Teresa? Don't need any action at this point . . . don't need jeopardy per se. Must keep in mind that Dick Francis plays relationships very nicely without jamming incessant screams and chases into the narrative.

3–13–89

I wonder if chapter nine will last all the way to Santa Teresa. What does Kinsey do when she gets home? She'll call Irene to make sure Agnes has arrived, which she will very soon. She'll introduce Dietz to Henry Pitts who'll be briefed about the situation re: the hit man. Security measures (if I knew what they were. . . .)

Want to dovetail "A" & "B" plots so both won't come in a ragged stop simultaneously.

Within a day, Agnes Grey will have disappeared from the nursing home.

Soon after, her body will be found.

Haven't quite solved the problem of how Kinsey gets hired to track down the killer.

Can't quite decide what the next beat is in the attempt on Kinsey's life. Dietz will get her a bulletproof vest. Does he jog with her? She won't really feel like it and he'll advise against. He'll have her take a different route to the office & home every day . . . always in his company.

Maybe Dietz has to make a quick trip to Carson City . . . or someplace. Papa sick? Mama sick? An unavoidable personal emergency. If I played my cards right, his absence might coincide with Kinsey's second trip to the desert. I guess I'll map all this out as I get to it but it does feel like a tricky business to make the story move smoothly through here.

Why do I worry so much about boring the reader? I don't want it to look like I've sacrificed the mystery and the pace for mere romance.

And skipping ahead to August . . .

8–12–89

Trying not to panic here. In the dead of night, Right Brain suggested that maybe Kinsey gets locked in the very storage bin Agnes was locked in. Nice claustrophobic atmosphere.

As a reader, I don't object to being privy to the reasoning process a detective goes through as long as it makes sense to me and seems logical. When the leap comes too fast, then I object. I like for the detective to consider every possible alternative.

My problem here is one of transitions . . . forging the links between the scenes I know are coming up.

8–15–89

Book was due today but so be it. Just closed out Chapter 23 and opened 24. I'm going to write notes to myself for a while and then print pages 30–35 so I can have them handy.

Need to set up "It used to be Summer . . ."

Maybe Kinsey & Dietz go back to Irene's & confront her with the true information on the birth certificate. If these aren't my parents, then who am I?

8–16–89

God, I'm tired today. I'd really love to sleep. Let's see what I can accomplish in a stupor. Can't wait for this book to be over and done.

Dear Right Brain,

Please be with me here and help me solve and resolve the remaining questions in the narrative. Help me to be resourceful, imaginative, energetic, inventive. And patient.

Look forward to hearing from you.

Sincerely,

Sue

I could pull up countless other samples, but you get the point I'm sure.

One comfort I take from my journals is that regardless of where I am in the current private eye novel, I can always peek back into the journals I've kept for previous books and discover that I was just as confused and befuddled back *then* as I am today. Prior journals are reminders that regardless of past struggles, I did somehow manage to prevail. Having survived through two novels, or five, or even twelve, in my case, there's some reason to suppose that I'll survive to write the next.

If you haven't already incorporated a journal or its equivalent into your current bag of writing tricks, you might try your hand at one and see how it works for you. Remember, it's your journal and you can do it any way you choose. If you don't use a PC, you can write yours in crayon on the ten-by-fourteen-inch sheets of newsprint. You can type it, write longhand, use a code if you need to feel protected. You can log in every day or only once a week. You can use it as a launching pad and then abandon the practice, or use it as I do, as an emotional tether connecting me to each day's work.

To help you get started, I'll give you the first entry just to speed you on your way:

Enter today's date.

Just sitting down here to try my hand at this weird stuff Sue Grafton has been talking about. A lot of it sounds like California psychobabble, but if it helps with the writing, who really cares?

In the book I'm working on what worried me is . . .

ON MEETING
YOURSELF

Robin Hemley

I know the exact moment—time, date, and place—I started to keep a journal: Wednesday, November 13, 1974, at 7:15 P.M. I was sixteen years old, and away at a St. Andrew's boarding school in Sewanee, Tennessee. The journal, thin and bright red, had the word "Record" imprinted on the cover. The price sticker was still on the inside:

STEELE'S $1.89

On the cover page I requested in big block letters that anyone who found my journal should please return it to my mother's address in South Bend, Indiana. (Above that are the mysterious words "Scorpion, elephant," not some secret code I'm sure, but hurried jottings, notes to myself on some poem (that's what I was writing back then) I thought would be published in the *New Yorker*, no doubt.

Now, the journal entry seems none too remarkable, but it's my first, my virgin journal entry in more ways than one—and at least shows what preoccupied me—namely, being a virgin.

> Walking from Mr. Feaster's house, overheard Beverly and Kurt talking.
> Bev: Everyone does it, you know.
> Kurt: (while chewing gum) Does what?
> Bev: Everyone tries to look sexually appealing.

Details are what interest the journal writer, no matter how one keeps a journal. Details are the minutiae of life we want to keep. All writers are observers who are fascinated with human goings-on, but journal writers are a special breed—suspicious of their own memories, like tourists taking snapshots of everything they see. They are different from diarists who are fascinated with their own lives. Journal keepers are snoops, enthralled with everyone else's life.

I don't think I've looked at that first entry more than once or twice before today. I'd pretty much forgotten about it, but I think it's fitting that my first entry was an overheard fragment of dialogue. In the years since the first page, I've filled my journal with similar bits of dialogue and anything else that struck me as unusual. My journal, however, is not only a compendium of observations, collected for the sake of record keeping, but also a writer's sketchbook, a place to try out ideas. I have included plot outlines, story ideas, character sketches, anecdotes that have been told to me, dreams, images, diarylike episodes—and the occasional grocery list.

I love the feel of a journal—the hard-shelled ledger variety especially (and they're getting more and more difficult to find. Who keeps ledgers anymore by hand?). I find that when I carry my journal, things worthy of being recorded seem to pop up all around me, which leads me to suspect, of course, that these things are always happening around me. I'm just more observant when I have my journal with me. There are times when it's not practical for me to carry a large journal, and so I almost always carry a pocket-sized notebook and a pen for those times. I believe it's crucial to write down my observations or thoughts in my journal the moment these observations occur. As Thoreau wrote, "The writer who postpones the recording of his thoughts uses an iron which has cooled to burn a hole with." That's a quote I wrote down in one of my journals. Otherwise, I'm sure I wouldn't have remembered it.

This is fairly typical of the way I work from my journals. Whatever fascinates me or at least holds my attention, I write down. These are the kernels for my writing, though I'm not saying that everything I write down needs to appear in a story or essay—or should. I also use my journal later in the process, for the research on a story, if it's needed, or for blocking out scenes or character sketches.

To me, everything we write is an exercise of sorts, and I'm using the word *exercise* loosely here to mean something that one throws out to the world in the spirit of experiment and invention. Of course, this is often when I write my best work, when I'm not trying too hard to make *Art*. My teacher in graduate school, Barry Hannah, used to tell us with seeming unselfconsciousness that he was going home after class to write *Art*.

But the way he said it with his Alabama accent and a certain impish smile made it seem like some game he was indulging in, made art seem not so serious. That's the way I most like to approach my work, as though I'm getting away with something, and that's why a journal works for me.

Last year, I took a group of my nonfiction students to France for a writing workshop, and I asked them to write a kind of travel exercise known as a lapidary—an odd name for a writing exercise, as *lapidary* is a term for working with gemstones, and the point of the exercise is to avoid being "polished." Apparently, Victor Hugo was a fan of this method, a kind of hurried and impressionistic travel sketch. The idea is to record your first impressions of a place as quickly as possible, avoiding the filter of self-consciousness. Some might call such an exercise a "lyric essay," but some people seem to call *anything* that isn't narratively driven a lyric essay. I prefer to say it's an exercise rather than invest it with too much importance. We're often so goal-oriented, so concerned with the end result of publication that we have difficulty allowing something to exist on its own. I suppose you could publish a collection of lapidaries, just as you might publish your journals if you were famous enough.

My journal is full of unpolished lapidaries and therefore has always been meant mostly for an audience of one. I'm simply snatching a moment, a phrase, a detail that otherwise would have been forgotten, and telling myself, here, remember this because it might be *Art* . . . someday. But not now.

I suppose I should add that over the years, as the direction of my writing has changed, so have my journals. I started out as a poet and most of my journals from when I was sixteen and seventeen contain my poems. Most of these poems are predictably self-conscious, purposefully written to posterity. I'm not horrified or amused by the poems. I simply don't want to read them because I remember them all too clearly and don't need to be reminded of how dreadful they are.

I do, however, want to read the little overheard bits of dialogue, and such, that I recorded almost as an afterthought. These really get at who I was at the age of sixteen in a way that my sixteen-year-old poems never can. The poems are simply examples of role-playing, trying on my identity as "Writer." But the little lapidaries of my life I made then, without a nod toward posterity are the ones that hold the most power for me. I don't pretend that any of these jottings will outlive me or hold any importance for anyone else, but for me they're better than photographs. They're photographs of my mind and they help me make a kind of sense of my development as a person as well as of my development as a writer.

Happily for the world, and me, I stopped writing poetry in my journals. Ever since then, my journals have been a place to record impressions of the world as I encountered it.

From my early twenties to my mid-thirties, I considered myself almost exclusively a writer of fiction, and my journals reflected this self-identity. Several short stories sprang from journal entries and a couple from dreams I recorded. In one dream, I was digging a hole in my backyard. Like many of my dreams, it had an absurd element. I remember that the hole I dug had a name, something like Fred or Jim. In the story, I took that part out and started to write a story in which a man goes to his ex-wife's backyard and starts digging a hole. She confronts him and asks him to stop, but he keeps digging. The fun of the story for me was in finding out why the man was doing this. I didn't know when I began. And I also wanted to make the story believable, to start out with this dreamlike element but give it some currency in the real world.

The other day, I was chatting with someone in my office when I mentioned that at the age of nineteen I had heard Maya Angelou deliver two lectures on consecutive nights in the seventies at the American Film Institute when my mother was a fellow there for a year. I remember sitting in the front row writing down just about every word she said. On the second night, she called me over and asked me who I was, tickled, I think that I was taking notes, and maybe a bit annoyed that no one else was. She gave me her address and said I should write her, saying I was like "everyone's little brother." I was flattered but I didn't write to her for twenty years (I have a bit of a procrastination problem), and by that time I was not "everyone's little brother," nor did I ever get a reply (although maybe she's got a procrastination problem, too). I was no longer the person she wanted to hear from, nor was she really the person I wanted to write to anymore. Both of us were contained in a fragmented but still potent way within that old ledger of mine.

As I chatted with the person in my office, I mentioned going to these lectures of Maya Angelou when I was young, and I quoted her as saying that one should be proud of one's work, but humble. Not earth-shattering advice, but still important for writers to keep in mind. In other words, it's okay to think of one's writing as *Art* and to be proud of your hard work, but not to go around trumpeting your *Genius*.

All my journals were right there on a shelf, and so I decided to see if I could find my original notes on Maya Angelou's lectures, which I hadn't looked at in nearly thirty years. I found them almost instantly, and to my surprise and delight, rereading the journal notes confirmed my memory. I don't think I would have remembered the lecture in the first place, at least not in so much detail, if I hadn't brought my journal with me on that night in 1977.

As I write this, I'm sitting in an apartment in Osaka, Japan, a place I haven't been since 1976 as an exchange student at a sister school, St. Andrew's. I'm here for a book I'm writing entitled *Do Over!*, in which, for a period of a week or so, I'm revisiting various sites of my childhood and in a sense doing them over. In the course of this project, I've spent the better part of a week back at summer camp, reprised a role from a school play in which I had flubbed a line, went back to kindergarten, and now have revisited both St. Andrew's and Momoyama (St. Andrew's in Osaka is called Momoyama). I wonder if I ever would have thought of this idea had I not been a journal keeper? I doubt it.

Returning to these various places of my youth has been moving and enlightening as well as odd and funny. When I returned to St. Andrew's, I felt like a grown up version of the person I had hoped to become while a student there, at least in terms of my profession. And I was still using a journal, but now as a kind of reporter's notebook, not so interested in awful poetry anymore, but still writing down overheard dialogue.

Like any resident student, I stayed in a dormitory room during my "do-over stay" at St. Andrew's. One day early in the week, there was a knock at my door. The teen boys in the next room wanted to invite me over and get to know me a bit.

"When did you graduate?" asked one of the boys. We sat on beds and on the floor while rock music from my era blasted out of the window.

"1976," I said.

"1976! You're young."

"I'm old," I said.

"No, you're still young," the kid said. "My dad graduated in 1971."

"But we're younger," one of the other boys said, and he and the first high-fived one another.

"You're reliving it," he told me, "but we're living it."

True, but at least when I went back to my room I thought to write it down. There's nothing wrong with a little reliving from time to time. That, in part, is what art does, and what journals help art accomplish.

To me, one either writes in a journal or one doesn't. They're not for every writer, and I don't think they should be shoved down anyone's throat. The only important rule in journal keeping is that you should *always* keep your journal in one of those fine and rare hardbound ledgers, not a three-ring binder or one of those flimsy college notebooks with the wire rings. And certainly not on your computer! In this computer-addled age, it's nice to carry around something tangible that links one directly to the joy of writing in one's own lousy penmanship, rather than generate a collection of neurons to be auto-saved on one's hard drive every fifteen minutes. It's nice to have a book to carry around, one that feels permanent and unique, unable to be duplicated, the nexus where the writer meets himself again, if not the rest of the world.

Kim Stafford

Poet of the Small Place

Born on an island, you long to venture
to the smaller island, more remote and
strange. Distant metropolis has no call
as piercing as the gull's cry when tide
threatens to dash the tiny craft you step
from, struggling toward obscurity
that alone will let you speak syllables
pried from the hid heart bone.

Kim Stafford

In my experience as a writer, there are two kinds of infinity: the constant local arrival of the intuitive, which gets put down in the notebook in my pocket; and the occasional recording of thoughts, which find their place in a folder on my computer. In general, the hand-wrought notebook gets the poetry; the machine gets the prose. The notebook is for my use in the life of creation; the computer files are for shared use in the life of conversation and collaboration with others—in Australia, Alaska, Scotland, and Oregon.

The Notebook in My Pocket

The notebook, the field book, the journal—the private, handheld prelude to typewriter or computer or anyone's eyes but my own—is the location for my own first handshake with the infinite.

The notebook should be small—shirt-pocket size, the size of the palm. The reason is suggested by one definition of poetry: Any utterance that sings in short space. To sing, we need all the resources of language—sound, rhythm, beauty, and toughness. The tighter the arena for the wild dance, the greater our sense of no limit. We seek a few words with boundless promise.

Sometimes in class, a student will put a few words together, and I feel a rush of envy. A student writes, "As a child, I was a swimmer—my only way to handle armloads of tears." We all sit stunned. "There is no limit," I say, "to what you could do with that." A writer's infinity is not time without end, but a brief time—a minute, a day, a lifetime—with too great an abundance of vitality and story. If you embrace the particular intensities that are yours, you will be blessed with hard work you may learn to cherish.

Sometimes, looking back, I find phrases in my notebook, a few words that recall some tremendous story, epoch, and understanding. I cherish those little signposts:

—the whole rhythm of water arguing softly with the ways of men
—"turn and look at your village"
—the times when we had songs for supper
—the moment when I touch my daddy's hat

As a writer, I find in these fragments abrupt doorways to the infinite. For example, that moment I picked up my father's hat, just before the woman I was to marry came into my house for the first time, the sentence went through my head, "My daddy got out of the way so this could happen."

Then there was the phrase in my notebook: "the times when we had songs for supper"—a reference to the Great Depression, a time of such privation for my family that its stories cast a light through life ongoing, like evening sun through the orchard. To have songs for supper instead of food is one extremely compact way to characterize a time of both hunger and glory. I can look and look into the little room of that phrase and never run out of all the stories whispering there.

In my notebook the phrase "'turn and look at your village'" comes to me from my Alaskan friend, the Inupiat artist Joe Senungetuk from the tiny village of Wales, north from Nome, where he grew up. He told me of his fourth-grade teacher there, Mrs. Coonz, back in the 1950s, taking the class on a field trip into the arctic darkness, leaving the school and walking two by two through the deep cold to the hilltop above, and then saying, "Turn around now, children, and look at your village."

Joe says in that moment, consciously turning to look at his village for the first time, he became an artist. He saw the work that was his to do. All my life, I will repeat that action, as I turn and look at my own village—my neighborhood, my city, my place on earth. The record of the story is a phrase in my notebook, put there so the seed can grow. Six words and no limit.

The hint in my notebook about "the whole rhythm of water"? What is that about? Carved on a stone by the river in my hometown is a line from my father's writing: "Water is always ready to learn." My father, the poet William Stafford, was magnetically drawn toward moving water. We were raised by rivers. The human equivalent to the rhythm of water, for me, is the daily rhythm of entering little discoveries into my notebook. The whole rhythm of the writing hand argues softly with the ways of men, and the ways of silence, violence, and injustice. The river, like the writer, keeps seeking the meeting place with other waters, on and on.

I call such phrases in the notebook miniature infinities, windows to stars, crevices glimpsed, inhaled, barely heard, never forgotten. Writing— especially in a notebook small enough to welcome "small" ideas—is my way to identify them and give them a chance to grow.

My students once gave me a fancy journal—leather bound, hand sewn—but I have never had an idea worthy of the book. I prefer the small notebook that welcomes all.

One time, during a concert in Nevada, the voice of Tish Hinojosa held us at attention, alert and amazed. She suddenly disappeared like smoke into an old song, *La Llorona,* that lifted me out of the world. I forgot my friends, my needs, my fears, everything. In that moment I understood a new kind of geometry in which my soul must dwell: life has a beginning, and an end, but no ceiling, and no ground. Within this brief span, we each may travel our boundless stories of ravishing grief and delight. There is no limit.

The words of the song, although greatly mysterious, were not the cause. The beauty of the voice, though exquisite, was not it. The age of the song, its anonymous origin in someone long gone, its connection to the tragedy of a whole people, its merciless beauty—perhaps was the cause. The song possessed me, and lifted me into a realm with no horizon and no circumference.

I looked at my friends beside me. I do not think they knew. I looked into the face of Tish Hinojosa, so talented and so young. I'm not sure even she knew the power of her song. She carried something she did not fully understand. May I do so! I looked ahead through my life to the end. It seems as if there is much good work to do. No limit.

Tápame con tu reboso, Llorona,	Cover me with your shawl, Llorona,
porque me muero de frío.	because I die of cold.
Dos besos que llevo en	Two kisses I wear on my face,
la frente, Llorona,	Llorona,
que no se apartan de mí:	may never leave me:
El último de mi madre, Llorona,	The last my mother gave, Llorona,
y el primero que te dí.	and the first I gave to thee.

In my life as a writer, it is precisely at such a moment when the notebook is my closest, most understanding friend. Dear human companions can't yet understand what I have seen . . . and the explaining, the wrestling for meaning—by poem, song, essay, story, manifesto—is somewhere in the future. In this moment, however, I can put a few words into the notebook, this smallest, most intimate, most mysteriously sophisticated time machine available to take me back to this moment of illumination from wherever I may stray as time moves on.

The File on My Computer

During moments every day like a weather-watcher I sense a gathering storm of correspondences that I would be a fool to ignore. Conversations, patches of yearning thoughts, recent dreams, a chance remark by someone nearby that frightens or invites me—these gather and begin to represent a cold front moving in, or an advancing episode of sudden spring. It's a twinge that quietly signals the need to gather considerations and see how they connect, how they reach, what they do.

When this happens, I take to the computer in my bag, because what's waiting is not a thread but a flood. The pocket notebook is for the hint, the computer for the deluge. The notebook is for the first move, an interlocking sequence of poetic lines—a fragment with rhythm, voice, and atmosphere whispering in my ear. The computer is for the encyclopedic mass of resonant data impinging deliciously on the mind.

The computer journal will let me wallow, if that is what I need to do, but the act of writing lifts me out. The facility of the computer keyboard enables me to reach in multiple directions quickly—a dream a decade old, a survey of possessions, a consideration of good chance or a challenge. And again, from this passage on the day of its creation, I find myself pasting language into another document—this time a personal writing plan as a companion to the budget plan I am preparing for my job. The journal on my laptop's hard drive is the chapter in invisible ink for the plan I will give to the college dean.

Sometimes, I take a journey, to feed a writing project I already have in hand. When I heard that the librarian at my late father's high school in Kansas had decided to dedicate her domain to two graduates who had become writers—William Stafford and B. H. Fairchild, leading her to name the school library the Stafford-Fairchild Library—I knew I had to attend the ceremony. Once there, I began gathering information like mad on the computer in my bag.

Below are three computer journal entries, the first one being most recent:

17 October 2004

The journey to Liberal, Kansas, which began as a formality, a dedication of the "Stafford-Fairchild Library," became a quest with the extra day the drive over prairie, the night and morning visits to the Cimarron . . . and then conversations with Pete Fairchild, wanderings, connections. But what have I learned?

William Stafford in high school seems to have been a shy, non-assured person in tight circumstances. A teacher got him to words (Miss Arrington), and with words he recovered a sense of self and a place in society. (Imagine him going through the privations and isolation of the war without a sense of being a writer.)

Just the glimpse of him in the graduation photo—in company with his narrator in "The Osage Orange Tree"—suggests a person very much at the edge of incapacitating shyness. Like my brother. My father, my brother, and I each began with a limited sense of belonging. My father and I found words—we could make something out of nothing, and this artifact had the power to move others, and by this we had something negotiable in the world. My brother didn't have this. What does this mean? Do word artifacts really amount to identity?

My brother is gone, and my father, and I think I have figured out how to be a human being. At heart, it isn't the negotiations in the human world that I am about—it is the moment in the marsh when the blackbirds fly . . . turning fifty-five anonymous in a prairie town

... meeting Lois and reaching back to the time of mystery . . . wandering in the cemetery at dusk . . . driving north out of town in the dark. Poetry gives visible evidence that confirms my life as mystic seeker, boy, wanderer, Ishi.

The writing life confirms the importance of my own experience to me. That's what it's about. The word-artifacts that result from this search are crumbs of bread that lead me back to dawn.

A geographical journey may be to a place that teaches you. The computer welcomes the abundant transfer of this experience to an archive for future use. Once I get home from my visit to the little prairie town where my father attended high school at the depth of the "dirty thirties," I have this trove of sensations connected to ideas which will form the matrix for multiple uses—writing, reconsidering my job, watching the growth of our son in a new way.

Here is another computer journal entry made the year before.

16 October 2003

I don't know what I'm doing. I pontificate as a teacher, I flounder as a traveler, I turn away from true creation as a writer, I have a faint grasp of my real duties on the job, and I'm present intermittently as a father, letting the precious days and years of our son's life slip through my fingers, the presence of my daughter in the world tumble farther from my presence. When does my wife see me? When do I see myself?

Why do it this way? Is the root problem my confidence that I can do all that comes toward me, and so I promise the world and myself too much, and I churn in frenzy and miss connection? Class tonight: I babbled, let people talk a little which moved us along to the next thing like climbing a ladder through time, rather than entering a meadow out of time. Three hours feels so short to me—what can we really get done? I've lost the ability to see the magnitude of such a workshop session, "the illusion of infinite time."

Here's another even earlier entry from my computer-based journal in 1995:

As I walked home from the college, through the green of the wood at evening, I understood that my wife and I would live in our small house for some years, perhaps always. I understood that my work at the college would not become easier, or better supported by the administration. I understood that my father's papers would take a great deal of energy, and would be an emotional challenge within the context of the family. I understood that my sister would not tell me the secrets that distance her, nor my mother embrace the parental work that belongs to her. I understood that important conversations with my former wife would never become easy or supportive of our daughter's inner growth. I understood that there would not be much money, and that I would take up all paying work that presented itself. I understood that my own writing would be done slowly, and only with great difficulty, in the small spaces I could find. I understood that somewhere in the midst of these difficulties, never to be completed, my life would end.

By the time I reached home, the little house where my wife was cutting up garlic in the kitchen, and out the window the hazel tree blazed in its greatest glory of green against the low sun, I understood how it felt to be ready, and to be free.

Much comes at you as a writer—myriad languages of word and memory, dream, sensation, instinct—with no limit to what you might do as a writer with all of this. The journal is the hinge between two infinite realms, the meeting place, the pivot. The journal in the pocket or on the hard drive is the arena for first apprehension, for private considerations of arrangement. From the darkness comes treasure, into the little light in hand comes composition, and into the darkness again go stories.

A writer has ambidexterity—to scribble by hand in a tiny notebook, or to use a computer to connect with friends and strangers far away. Gutenberg's moveable type can now move a tiny story across the globe. Gutenberg started, however, by printing the Bible, a work of tremendous substance. Our work now is to develop new content worthy of the new tool—to craft e-mail messages that make readers weep, or laugh, or change. The joining of the notebook and the computer is an intercultural marriage. We are all growing up in this lively household.

My sense of the modern shifted when I realized the computer screen is the size of a folksong. What we once composed orally now fits neatly on the lit face of the box. Something very old is about to happen in a new way.

Ilan Stavans

Keeping a notebook is a way to trust myself. Over the years I've accumulated a number of them and still see them as chapters of the same endeavor. They are usually Mead Composition books, 100 sheets or 200 pages, 9 ¾-by-7 ½-inch / 24.7-by-9.0 cm, wide ruled.

I mostly write in longhand. Somehow, I feel this old-fashioned method allows me to be more in touch with certain currents of thought in my mind. A plethora of ideas emerge at any point during my day. The question is, which are worth writing down and which are not? The only way to find out is to stamp them on a notebook page, to see them relate to one another.

I am known for writing all the time: morning, afternoon, and evening. But I only devote the late hours of the night to my notebook. I start writing it when I'm exhausted and all other duties have been completed. It's good to have my defenses down.

In my notebook I use any pencil or pen at my disposal, whatever color. I seldom compose full-fledged paragraphs. Instead, I do all sorts of tricks. I might note the title of a book I want to read, or someone's telephone number on the upper corner of the page, or I might paste in old postcards and photographs (à la W. G. Sebald), as well as newspaper clippings. Or I might draw a doodle.

The technique I use in my notebook writing is akin to creating marginalia. I don't write in straightforward fashion but in waves. An idea shows up and becomes a line. I then cross it out and put another one on top, add several below or on the side, and so on. I let myself enjoy non sequiturs.

To others my notebook might appear to be a messy, incoherent affair. Besides, I don't like my notebook to be read by strangers. To me the accretion of material (in Talmudic fashion) distills truth. Truth is what literature is about: the conviction that through words, not just any words but *the right* words, and whatever else accompanies them, I might reach the essence of things.

While browsing through my notebook (and I do it often, at different hours of the day), I realize there are plenty of lists—to-do lists, lists of students' names, lists of archaic words. Here's a list of my books about to be published or those which are on the front burner:

The Norton Anthology of Latino Literature (anthology)
Mr. Spic Goes to Washington (graphic novel, with Roberto Weil)
American Immigrant Writing (anthology)
Gabriel García Márquez: A Biography (2 vols.)
With All Thine Heart (book-long Q&A, with Mordecai Drache)
César Chávez: A Pictorial (young adults)
Twentieth-Century Latin American Poetry (anthology)
Borges and the Jews (book-long essay)
Hispanic Anti-Semitism (book-long essay)
Rebellion in the Backlands, by Euclides Da Cunha (introduction)
Remapping La Hispanidad (book-long Q&A, with Iván Jaksic)

Sometimes these lists become an end in and of themselves. I never return to them in the notebook. However, on most occasions, each of the items listed acquires an independent status at a later date.

For the purpose of explaining how I use my notebook in my literary life, I will follow one example. My notebook was essential in shaping my graphic novel *Mr. Spic Goes to Washington.* It was in its pages that I first conceived the project. There is an entry that reflects on two words that struck me: *Spic* and *Span:* "I could use them as names in a Marx Brothers parody."

I listed some possible titles for this parody: *Spic and Span at the Bullfight* or *Spic and Span Dancing Salsa.*

Next I discarded Span and kept Spic. I wrote: "A graphic novel with Spic as protagonist?" There are lines about a possible plot: Spic is described mestizo, a gang member with several deaths on his conscience. I began to think of Art Spigelman's *Maus I* and *II.* "Nooooo," the notebook argues, "it needs to be more contemporary." Several pages later I imagined Spic's adventure as a cautionary political tale. "Maybe a parody of the 1939 movie *Mr. Smith Goes to Washington*, with Jimmy Stewart." Within a few pages, the novel's title spontaneously came to me.

Some notes on renting the DVD of Frank Capra's movie were then recorded in my notebook. I downloaded the movie poster, printed it, and then stapled it on a page. I then wrote about a restless night, trying to reconcile sleep while thinking about the plot. "A critique of ethnic politics in twenty-first-century U.S."

In my notebook, I was able to come to terms with what came next. I wrote an e-mail to my friend and one-time collaborator, Lalo López Alcaraz, with whom I did a cartoon book, *Latino USA*. He loved the idea and suggested I approach Spic as S.P.I.C., an acronym for Samuel Patricio Inocencio Cárdenas. A provocative response!

I began to explore some scenarios, such as, Spic in East L.A., Spic at the Jefferson Memorial in Washington, D.C., Spic at the Senate. "A comedy?" I wasn't sure where the plot was taking me. I imagined it would be ninety pages. Looking for a cartoonist to collaborate with (at the time, Alcaraz, a top choice, was going through a nasty divorce and struggling with substance dependency) would be a challenge. "Ninety pages: a manageable number," I wrote in my journal.

Now that I am going through my journal, I notice a short list of names of potential cartoonists. Before I contacted anyone, I wrote several pages of content in my notebook. It came to me fast and furiously. In fact, I have a note to myself that I wrote it in two hours. I don't think the verb *to write* is even appropriate. I felt as if the material was dictated to me from above.

In my notebook, I made some doodles (of course, none good enough to become part of the book): a muscular Spic, Spic with mustache and bandana, Spic with a tattoo. Next to one I penciled: "Yes, mucho humor!"

I penciled in some thoughts about an e-mail conversation I had around that time with Richard Nash, the editor in chief of Soft Skull.

I wrote, "Richard has been recommended to me by Bob Arellano."

Bob Arellano, a Cuban American writer in New Mexico who was educated at Brown, was then doing a graphic book himself, which he asked me to blurb. I responded positively and suggested I might want to do one myself and he suggested that I speak to Richard.

Arellano led me to two of the three artists he had worked with. I interviewed them and in my notebook I detailed a conversation with one of them: "He seems difficult. Will something come out of it?" I didn't explain it any further, but the connection with that artist (inflexible and snobbish) went nowhere.

Some pages later, I stated that my Boston friend, Gerardo Villacres who is on the editorial board of the newspaper *El Planeta,* as well as his colleague Javier Marin, recommended Roberto Weil, a syndicated cartoonist from Caracas. I printed some of Weil's images from the Web, pasted them into my notebook, and wrote comments around them.

I met Weil via e-mail. There is nothing in the notebook about my first electronic encounter with him, nor about the type of relationship we eventually forged. I devoted space to other interests, such as a play called *The Disappearance* based upon my short story and the drafting of my biography about Gabriel García Márquez. I then returned to the content of the graphic novel. I polished the material I had already written, then speculated on its value before sending it to Weil.

Here's one segment from my journal:

Page 15 [three panels]: Panel A: A line at the bottom reads: "Senator Samuel Patricio Inocencio Cárdenas arrives at Ronald Reagan Airport." Spic is carrying suitcases. He has his big crucifix hanging from his chest. His T-shirt has a quote: "I know you're here to kill me. Shoot, coward! You're only going to kill a man—Ernesto 'Che' Guevara." Panel B: seated in a taxi (the Capitol is in background) while talking to the Pakistani cab driver. Spic asks the driver: "Many foreigners in the capital?" The driver responds: "No one is a native in America any more!" Panel C: Spic leaving a grocery store named Easy Mart. Spic thinks, "No hay chiles. Las tortillas son de plástico. Jesús, why have you forsaken me?"

In my notebook I added: "Ask Roberto if the image is too cinematic. Can he make it look as reminiscent? Am I thinking these images in the right way? What's the difference between a graphic novel and a screenplay? And what's the difference between writing a novel and writing a graphic novel? It has to be dramatic. Anyway, wait for his answer."

Here's another segment:

Page 63 [two panels]: Panel A: In his delirium, Spic falls asleep. He is visited by "Che" Guevara. Che Guevara says: "I don't care if I fall as long as someone else picks up my gun and keeps on shooting." Then there's apparitions of Abraham Lincoln, who says: "I'm a firm believer in the people. If given the truth, they can be depended upon to meet any national crises. The great point is to bring them the real facts." And an apparition of Cesar Chavez, who says: "Love is the most important ingredient in nonviolent work." Spic says: "Jijole, is there a way to address Latino issues that isn't through radicalism? I thought I had left that strategy on campus years ago. And is there a significant leader in our community that isn't also a martyr? Death is always lurking in back. . . . Those that accept the status quo are ineffective. And those that don't are summarily eliminated in a blinker!" Panel B: Spic wakes up, although he's still in his sleep. He looks around: the Senate is filled with other historical figures: Fray Bartolomé de Las Casas, Thomas Jefferson, Emiliano Zapata, Noam Chomsky, Evita Perón, Fidel Castro, Hugo Chávez. Next to them are still Lincoln and Chavez.

The entry is followed by this line: "This might be too ethereal. Will the reader grasp the fact that Spic, as a character, is going through a crisis?"

Soon after, I seemed to have begun e-mailing portions of the content to Weil because more or less from this point on, *Mr. Spic Goes to Washington* was no longer mentioned in any detail in my notebook. I moved the gestation of the book out from its pages to a one-on-one relationship with Weil and, subsequently, with Nash, who ultimately acquired the graphic novel and published it in August 2008.

My notebook is the perfect space to experiment. Whenever a Mead Composition Book is complete, I store it away in a special place in a room on the third floor of my Amherst house, where I keep my correspondences, manuscripts, and other documents. I make sure to date the first page. The journals which I've quoted here span from May 2005 to March 2008. Often times, I pull out a notebook to see what I thought about an idea. This back-and-forth enables me to see how I conceived an idea.

And I buy another notebook. They are easy to find in any stationery store. Their black-and-white cover looks like a marble stone. (I bought the one I'm describing a while ago. It cost me $1.99 at CVS Pharmacy.)

I don't intend for my notebooks ever to published. I feel naked in them—comfortably naked, yes, but naked nonetheless.

A LIFE OBSERVED

Katherine Towler

Other girls kept diaries in little pink, leather-bound books with a gold lock and key. I kept a journal in a serviceable notebook that would tell anyone who saw me bent over it, scribbling away, that I was no casual writer. The summer I was eleven, I wrote, "to catch the thoughts as they flow" on the cover of my notebook and set it in a duffel bag beside my camp uniform. I was not interested in a diary about boys and parties, with a cover marked "private" or "keep out." I hoped to be a real writer one day.

Trinity Mountain Camp for Girls was run by the Sisters of Saint Margaret, an order of Episcopal nuns. In 1967, when their Catholic counterparts were shedding the habit and going out into the world in the flush of post–Vatican II freedom, these nuns remained covered from head to toe in wimple, veil, and black robes that brushed the grass as they strode toward the chapel in the ninety-degree heat. We were in awe of those severe women, not only of their ability to withstand the heat in so many layers of cloth, but also of their single-minded devotion to a religious calling. Some of the more devout campers joined the nuns for their private service of Compline. Other girls spoke of becoming nuns themselves. I was not among them. Though I loved the cadence of the prayers and the ritual of the services in the small chapel where we sat pressed close together in plain wooden pews, I was aware even then that I had another calling. My religion was writing.

While the other girls played foursquare on the blacktop outside the rec hall before lunch, I could be found under a tree, my journal propped in my lap, writing poems. I did not personally know any writers, but instinctively I had stumbled on the idea of keeping a journal, because I realized that this is what writers must do. I was not yet able to write whole pages that might add up to a story or (glory of glories) an entire book. The most I could sustain were bits of poems, random collections of lines, short reflections. The concept of finishing a piece of writing, taking it through successive drafts, did not yet exist for me. I reveled in the heady pleasure of committing a few words to paper and treasured each like a rare jewel I had dug from the earth with my bare hands. A journal suited my fledgling status as a writer and made me feel serious and important, a real writer, and honored the scant output I produced. In my journal I practiced being a writer in both senses of the word: practiced as in trying out, and practiced as in keeping a daily practice, the way the nuns observed their daily order of prayer services.

From an early age, I was a passionate and constant reader, far more interested in curling up on the couch with a good book than in going outside to play. I adored words and what words arranged on a page could accomplish in the mind of a reader, painting vivid pictures, conjuring up exotic places, and making imagined people come to life with a force that real, live people often seemed to lack. At the same time, writing was what I used to separate myself from others, to define myself as different, and the notebook with the brown cardboard cover that served as my journal was the potent symbol of what set me apart. There was arrogance in this, and a determined longing.

From the start of my efforts to become a writer, I had a love / hate relationship with the whole business. I wanted more than anything to be seen as someone with a special talent that marked me as one of the chosen few who had risen from the ranks of the ordinary. I also wanted, desperately, to be accepted and liked, to belong and be included in the gang.

These two desires fought with each other at constant odds, a split in my nature that persists to this day. For a shy, skinny, and awkward girl, writing was a good place to hide. In the pages of my journal, I took comfort in the power of the words that I alone could fashion. The making of a private world in words sustained me and in a strange way protected me from the terrors of the rough and tumble world of people. Yet the very thing that appeared to be my salvation, giving a quiet girl who lived in her mind much of the time a way to be, set me further apart from others, exacerbating my sense of isolation. The journal in which I first practiced being a writer came to be a talisman of this fundamental divide in my character.

For Christmas one year when I was a teenager, my father gave me an old piece of sheet music he had found in an antique store. The song was titled "All Alone," and the cover featured a blurry black-and-white photograph of a young woman holding a hand to her breast and gazing mournfully into the distance. The gift was meant to be a playful joke. Everyone laughed when I ripped apart the wrapping paper and revealed the dreamy-eyed woman. "I thought she looked like you," my father said. He was right; the woman did bear a resemblance to me, or at least what I might have looked like had I been living in the 1920s. But the laughter of my mother and sisters came from recognition, not only of the long, thin lines of the woman's face, but also of the appropriateness of the song's title. I was "all alone," and spent hours in my bedroom reading and writing or up in the attic gazing out at the city rooftops stretching away to a slice of river.

In a picture taken of me when I was fifteen, I am standing on a lawn next to the building where we lived in a baggy pair of corduroy pants and a denim jacket, my frizzy hair hanging past my shoulders, the image of an early 1970s hippie child. In my hand I am holding a plain brown notebook—my journal. I was not all alone, because I took my journal with me everywhere, along with a camera. Photography became my other passion, and my journal and my camera became my means of capturing my experience of the world in a crafted form. My photographs and my journal pages were aimed at art, but I understood even then that the journals were not art. They were the trail markers for the art I would one day make.

In college, I continued to write sporadically in my journal, but I did not take any writing classes. Though writing remained a secret love, with the journal as my silent companion, I believed I might be headed for a career in photography. One night in the fall of my junior year, attempting to write a history paper in the stacks of the library, I became so bored that I picked up a stray copy of the college catalogue lying at the end of a nearby bookshelf. I sat and actually read the thing, and in doing so, discovered the existence of the New England Literature Program, or NELP as I would affectionately come to call it.

For six weeks in the spring, NELP took some thirty undergraduates to live in a camp on Lake Winnipesauke in New Hampshire. Guided by two wonderfully eccentric English professors, we read Thoreau, Dickinson, Emerson, and Hawthorne. Classes were conducted on the dock overlooking the lake or up in the field behind the cabins. We spent three days a week hiking in the White Mountains, and we were required to keep a journal of the whole experience. In their wisdom, our professors understood that academic papers would not suit the program, where reading the poetry of Robert Frost was of a piece with hiking the New England woods.

I came to NELP already a journal writer, but I left with a renewed and relentless passion for the blank pages in those blank notebooks. For the first time, I knew other people who kept journals and saw my journal as a recognized and legitimate form of writing. For the first time, I let someone else read my journal. Though we were allowed to mark pages of a personal nature we did not want read, I shared just about everything with my professors in my unabashed enthusiasm, causing them some embarrassment. They overlooked my too frank accounts of one unrequited crush and another brief affair. I am still in touch with one of the professors, now retired. He tells me that my NELP journals hold a record for being among the longest of any student's in the more than thirty years of the program's existence.

The permission I was given by my NELP teachers not only to write, but also to write in a journal, came at a key moment in my life and shaped me in ways that made a lasting difference. Halfway through the six weeks, when one of my professors read the pages I had written, he returned my journals with a handwritten letter that said, "Lurking behind these journal entries is an autobiographical novel of power and interest." Becoming a writer was no longer my private, secret dream. Someone else saw the possibility and believed in it, too. My NELP professors were on the cutting edge in the mid-1970s of using journals in the "classroom." Today the practice is ubiquitous, with everyone from first graders to graduate students routinely keeping journals of one sort or another. But when I went off to the New Hampshire woods, journaling was not yet an established trend in America. It came as a revelation to discover the value in the battered notebooks I had lugged around since I was eleven.

In the years that followed that first sanctioned experience of being a journal writer, I filled notebook after notebook. My journal accompanied me through the last year of college, when I was working in a camera store as I tried to figure out what came next, on a two-month trip around Europe with a Eurail pass, and through graduate school. In my journal I recorded the inconceivable loss of a young friend to cancer, the attempts to find love, my nightly dreams, and quotes from writers I admired. Though I wrote regularly and often at great length, with single entries taking up ten or more handwritten pages, my journal remained primarily a record of my emotional states, a place to write down thoughts and feelings rather than events. I became, like all writers, an observer of my own life, yet the life I was interested in observing was largely an internal one, the things I could not voice to others but reveled in voicing to myself.

To believe that you have something to say that the world is just waiting to hear, and that no one else can say it in quite the way you can, is self-centered, to say the least. But this is what we ask of artists, that they make a journey into the self and return to tell us what they have found. We are grateful to artists of all types (musicians, painters, dancers, actors) for spending the time in reflection, thought, and creative engagement, and then sharing the results. From early on in my practice of being a journal writer, I saw myself embarking on such a journey, traveling into the self and making a map of those uncharted depths. Here, I believed, was my best work. One day my journals would prove to be a lasting (dare I say brilliant?) record of a young woman's coming of age in the latter half of the twentieth century.

In many ways, my journals are my best work, though not as I once thought, for the intrinsic value of the pages themselves. By keeping a journal, I learned to be an observer of my own emotions and shifts in thinking and belief. I learned to look for patterns in my responses to my experiences. I came to understand myself as a being who changed over time. Writing an account of the ways I continually surprised and disappointed myself, of how I made the same mistakes over and over, of how I refused to learn the very lessons I set out to teach myself in my journal, made me question bedrock assumptions about myself. I was forced to acknowledge in the pages of my journal the gap between knowing something and being able to act on it. I was constantly reminded of my own flawed nature, of the essential blindness, willfulness, and selfishness that make us all human. This practice of trying to truly know and understand myself was what I drew on most when I began to write novels.

Twenty years after I received a master's degree in fiction writing from Johns Hopkins, I published my first book. For a long, long time (as it felt to me), I met strangers on airplanes and at parties and told them I was a writer and then had to respond to the inevitable question, "What have you published?" Nothing (or next to nothing)—a couple of short stories in little magazines that folded shortly after publishing my work didn't count. I was writing throughout these years, working on drafts of three different novels, and producing short stories and occasional poems. I was writing in my journal, page after handwritten page detailing my struggles with the novels and short stories, my discouragement and my fervent hope. My journal, more than anything else, carried me through these years, confirming on all those scrawled pages that I was, indeed, a writer.

After my first novel was published, I had the startling experience of hearing my work described by others who were not fellow writers in a writing workshop. Reviewers noted the sense of atmosphere and setting in my books. Readers at book events in bookstores and libraries spoke about the characters. These people put my writing in a context and named the different aspects of my work that had remained for me vague and unconscious. What came up again and again was the focus on character, not plot, as the driving force in my novels. Though surely I must have known this is what I was doing, I could not have identified it clearly until my books were out in the world with a life of their own. Then I understood how deeply this vein ran through my work.

For me, story always begins with character, with the shadowy images of imagined people who live in my mind. Wanting to know and understand these people keeps me writing. What happens to my characters is of consequence, but the essence of the undertaking is getting to know them on a deep and sustained level, living with them, listening to them, waiting for them to reveal themselves. This process requires patience and takes place over time, not days or weeks, but months and years, not unlike my own long journey of attempting to know myself through the pages of my journals.

You could say that it was my interest in character—my own and others'—that led me to become an ardent journal writer and later a novelist. Or you could say that the years of keeping a journal that charted my own growth and change led me to become a writer of novels with a strong focus on character. I cannot determine which came first, as the two were always entwined for me, the journal a reflection of my desire to do something more with writing, the novels a natural outgrowth of all that internal searching and reflection. Keeping a journal, however, was an essential piece of my training as a writer. By observing my own life, I learned to observe the lives of others.

I drew on my experience as a journal writer directly in my second novel and placed a fictional journal at the heart of the book. The journal is written by a woman who marries a fisherman and goes to live on a New England island in 1930. Her daughter finds the journal after her death. The narratives of the two women—the daughter in the 1960s and the mother in the found pages of her journal recording her life in the 1930s and 1940s—make up the alternating strands of the novel. In writing this fictional journal, I did not use any material from my own journals. I invented a voice and an unfolding story, trying to be true to a woman of that time who lived a hardscrabble life and endured a difficult marriage and gave birth to four children. I wrote Phoebe Shattuck's journal entries very much as I would write my own, though, as short, meditative pieces, completing only one or two entries in a morning as I attempted to capture the rhythm of a real journal. Often I felt so close to her that I was in a state akin to hypnosis, taking dictation from a far off voice that was at once disembodied and utterly real. This is the nearest I have come to an experience other writers have described as something like "channeling" a character or taking dictation from God. Phoebe Shattuck's journal seemed to write itself.

Writing Phoebe Shattuck's journal was a significant step that allowed me to translate my own long history as a journal writer into a fictional form. I suppose it is no coincidence that this step came about at a time of change in my habits as a journal writer, when I found myself writing far less in the pages of my marble-bound notebooks. Many published writers disdain journal writing as a self-indulgent and wasteful practice. Time spent writing in a journal is time that could be spent on short stories and novels and essays. Who cares about your dreams or the state of your marriage? Put that energy into the real work, they say, where it belongs.

I now have a good deal of sympathy for this point of view, though I would not have given it much credence in earlier years. Maybe it's partly a question of age. My life is more crowded and complicated now. I truly do not have time to write regularly in my journal, complete the draft of a novel, work as a teacher and freelance writer, and have any kind of a life beyond this. If writing in my journal were important to me, though, I could make the time, but I have to admit that it is not important to me, not in the ways it once was, and with this acknowledgement comes the equally clear insight that it is only because of my years of journal writing, my years of closely observing my own life, that I no longer need to continue the practice as I once did.

In the pages of my journal, I learned to live with contradictions and unresolved conflicts. I became more forgiving of myself, which helped me to become more forgiving of others. I paid attention to nuances in thought and feeling, the small shifts that added up to eventual understanding and change. I practiced compassion for my own confused state of being. Over time the act of journal writing, which began as such a self-absorbed and self-indulgent habit, made a leap of translation. I was finally able to see others as I saw myself, full of longings and regrets, joys and misgivings. I understood, at last, that I was no different from other people. Their feelings, I knew, were my own feelings. The notebooks that had preserved my sense of separateness for so long came to represent something else entirely—the record of what I shared with others as a human being searching for hope and meaning and guidance, trying to live with my own frustrations and failings.

My journal notebooks are lined up on a shelf in a corner of my office, under the edge of my desk. There are more than fifty notebooks of all shapes and sizes and colors collected over the years. I rarely take them off the shelf. Rereading them can be as painful as it is illuminating. I no longer fantasize about the day when they might be published. Instead, I imagine burning them, making sure they never fall into others' hands. I am not at all convinced, as I once was, that a significant historical record or brilliant writing lies between the pages of all those notebooks. I am convinced, though, that the writing of those pages taught me more than I will ever realize, that my years as a journal writer were essential to the work I am doing now, and to the work still to come.

BLOGGING LIKE A CHILD-ARSONIST

Tony Trigilio

The relationship between journaling and my own poems became apparent once I grew tired of apologizing for our lovely but deranged cat, Shimmy.

I had always been a prolific journaler, and like most writers, I tried to take my pen and notebook everywhere with me. As e-mail and word processing gradually took over my writing life, the time I had once devoted to pen-and-notebook journaling was now spent in daily correspondence with friends and fellow writers. Fragments from my letters found their way into poems. I used letters as I would a journal, as a staging area for new work. I read deeper into the published correspondence of my favorite writers—Emily Dickinson, George Oppen, Elizabeth Bishop, Henry Miller, Robert Duncan—and I discovered the beauty of tracing a writer's literary style back to the fierce, primal energy in the unguarded prose of their correspondence.

As a student and compulsive journaler, I worked in the Kent State Department of Special Collections under poet Alex Gildzen, and there I was drawn to the role of letter writing as an artist's form of journaling. I'll always be grateful to Alex for encouraging me to read the correspondence that I saved for future generations in acid free folders—especially the impressive, voluminous letters of filmmaker James Broughton and playwright Jean-Claude van Itallie. I learned the art of letter writing while reading those in the Special Collections and saw in the letters of poets that they *lived* the poems they were writing.

Journals offer nearly the same for me; but journals are often only a one-way mode of communication, whereas letters unambiguously presume a dialogue, an interlocutor listening and reacting immediately to what has been written. Letter writing, and reading the letters written by other writers, eventually became more of a thrill for me than reading my own journal and made it clear that my letters had taken over the intimate space once occupied by spiral-bound notebooks.

Three of the most important poems in the manuscript I'm working on, *Historic Diary*, based on the myths and texts of Lee Harvey Oswald, come directly from fragments of letters I'd written to friends: "What I Missed," "Dallas," and "Letter to Hilles from Lake Forest." This last one, from a letter to the poet Rick Hilles, is especially significant to my journaling and letter-writing history because it was Rick who introduced me many years ago to Richard Hugo's inventive epistolary poems in *Thirty One Letters and Thirteen Dreams*. My manuscript itself takes as its source text Oswald's journal composed in the Soviet Union, which he titled the *Historic Diary;* and in diary and epistolary formats, the poems reshape, with the trace of a child-vandal's energy, the correspondence taken from the shamefully tangled, obedient exhibits and reports prepared by the Warren Commission.

Still, despite this mapping of literary and historical influence, my repeated apologizing for Shimmy's destructive actions made all the difference in the relationship between my journaling and my poems.

When my wife, Shelly and I lived in Boston a decade ago, Shimmy attacked Andryc, the three-year-old son of a dear friend, who had come over specifically to see her. The boy yelled, "Kitty!"—no doubt enthralled that Shimmy resembled his own cat—and ran to pet her. Like any small creature concerned with self-preservation in the presence of a child, she fled. She galloped toward her favorite hiding spot beneath our living room couch, then stopped in mid-flight, and probably realized that this was her own home and Andryc was nothing more than a predatory intruder. Perhaps she retained an olfactory memory of the evening about two years earlier when Andryc's mother had changed his diaper on our bed—with Shimmy hiding beneath it. She stopped before the couch. Andryc reached toward her, arms outstretched in frightful, unmitigated joy. Shimmy poised back on her haunches and swung her front paw.

I watched and could see Shelly's eyes go wide. Shimmy's paw flashed. In slow motion, half-speed, with her pumpkin-colored fur leaving slow motion trails behind it, I saw her claws extend. Andryc's father, Mitch, did not know the power of Shimmy's rage. We had adopted her as a feral kitten lost in the woods, and she's never trusted anyone but Shelly and me. She took a cautious step forward and struck Andryc's arm. I watched her translucent claws sink into the blue vinyl and puffy goose lining of his winter jacket.

I quickly grabbed Shimmy and moved her to a safe distance from Andryc. In the brief silence before Andryc began wailing, Shimmy turned her head back toward him and hissed, her back legs flailing. We were lucky Andryc was wearing his winter jacket; the claws did nothing but puncture the lining. But as I mentioned later to Mitch, I felt as if we had witnessed and helped cause a primal trauma that Andryc would remember for a long time.

A few moments later, when everything calmed down and after Andryc had screamed, in heaving sobs, to his mother on the telephone, and I had apologized over and over—it occurred to me that for most of her life I had been apologizing for Shimmy.

"I don't know what to do sometimes," I said to Mitch. "It's like having a child who's an arsonist. You love her with all your heart, but you keep saying things to your neighbors like, 'I'm sorry Shimmy burned down your tool shed, and we'll pay all the damages.'"

This would be my operative apology over the years: *I'm sorry; she's crazy but we love her; it's like having a child who's an arsonist.* You want to help her live calmly in the world, but you cannot deny the trouble she causes everyone. She's a cat, after all, not a child, and she'll never domesticate completely—especially with her early, kitten memories of starving in the woods before she wandered into a friend's basement and we adopted her. Every action she undertakes will be uncensored, whether she's content or terrified.

And it's this untamable feral instinct that we've come to admire over the years, an enviable rage crucial to her survival those first few weeks of her life when she got lost from (or was abandoned by) her mother. Shimmy's child-arsonist persona was itself a sort of reminder of what lies unfettered inside us.

Our move from Boston to Chicago only made things worse for Shimmy. She hid under our bed for six weeks, no matter how lovingly we enticed her out with wet food. In correspondence, I found myself writing about her more and more. In long letters about new writing projects, or about my buffoonery trying to navigate a new city that seemed hundreds of times larger than Boston, I'd find myself closing with postscripts about my cat:

> P.S. Shimmy is staring at her catnip mouse. Just staring.
> [She later would scare a real mouse to death and sit proudly next to its upturned, unbitten body.]
> P.S. Shelly sometimes likes to take Shimmy into the hallway outside our new apartment. This is asking for trouble. If your child were a homicidal arsonist, would you take him / her to children's birthday parties? Shimmy loves smelling the carpet, where she can pick up the scent of the two dogs living above us. She stays in the hall, sniffing, for about five seconds, and then she remembers it's not our apartment and anything can happen in the outside world—and dogs live around her! She rushes like mad, tail up, back into our apartment to lick herself.
> [Anytime the upstairs neighbor came to say hello, or borrow detergent because he always seemed to run out, Shimmy would run maniacally down our hallway so fast that she'd lose control and slide on the hardwood floors hissing at him.]

Sometimes I even spoke in her voice at the end of letters. I knew I was treading on dangerous ground—talking in the voice of my cat. I had to trust, as my letter-writing friends did, that I never would become someone who bought kitten calendars and made oversize-JPG shrines on my website for my animal friend. I added a postscript once to my cousin, Michael, in a letter full of foaming-at-the-mouth vitriol about Kenneth Starr, a letter that later would provide material for my poem "Special Prosecutor," in *The Lama's English Lessons:* "Shimmy is upset because neither you nor anyone else we know rescued her from her vet checkup at the Den of Spies last week." Somewhere along the way, I had decided that Shimmy's name for the veterinarian's office was the Den of Spies, the name that Islamist radicals bestowed on the U.S. embassy in Iran when they attacked it in 1979. Shimmy in turn decided that her vet was not Dr. Beau, a caring doctor with the patience of a saint for treating our raving cat, but instead was Dr. Kissinger, the former secretary of state who, in Shimmy's mind, strutted around the Uptown Animal Hospital in a bloodstained butcher's apron.

I really scared myself during those moments when I switched into the voice of my cat: *Dr. Kissinger touched me all over, Michael, and you should have heard the rustic hacking of those mangy dogs—I wanted to strangle them with my bare hands.* Nothing particularly poetic or even eloquent. The plea to my cousin in the voice of my cat instead, was simply a raw, uncensored burst of prose like any other I would write, taking it or leaving it, in a journal or letter. I still kept a journal at this time, in a trusty spiral-bound notebook, but I composed my most instinctive, unfettered writing in letters to my friends.

Around this time, as Shimmy spoke in the postscripts of my letters, and my friends responded to both of us, humoring me and humoring themselves, I discovered poets' blogs. I use the word *discovered* here as if something magical occurred once I read the blogs of fellow poets. As if this were my version of John Keats feeling "like some watcher of the skies/ When a new planet swims into his ken," from his poem "On first looking into Chapman's Homer." It was nothing of the sort. I came to blogs, or entered the blogosphere, as it's often called, with no grand Keatsian expectations.

I realized that blogs were public versions of private journals. With millions of blogs on blogspot.com alone, odds were slim I would find much of Henry Miller's mad lyricism anywhere. Still, as I found more and more blogs written by poets, I assumed that I would be privy to the secret minute particulars of their creative processes—that blogs would reveal the hidden crawlspaces in the finished architecture of contemporary poems. Some of this was true, and the best example was Ron Silliman's brilliant near-daily blog postings on contemporary poetics (http://ronsilliman .blogspot.com). At the same time, most blogs seemed to be nothing but self-serving promotional tools, or, worse, diatribes against the hypocrisies of the "poetry business." God knows promotional blogs are useful; too often I've fallen into the trap of thinking that my work ends with publication, when actually this is when promotion begins. And I'd question the sanity of anyone who didn't find the poetry business cutthroat and repugnant. Still, it seemed blogs could do more for my writing process, and serve a purpose similar to diaries and notebooks.

I was struck by how the rich, journaling nature of blogging went untapped in the many metacritical takes on the poetry business I was reading in the blogosphere. Blogs seemed to combine the potential for both private, undomesticated journaling *and* public performance. Why else would one choose to distribute one's private journals in a forum, the World Wide Web, with a greater audience than any of the most highly circulated print poetry journals?

As much as I was drawn to Silliman's blog, I abhorred the sycophan-
tic stream of responses in the comments. Silliman's blog would sometimes
generate fifty to one hundred comments to an individual posting, most
of which nodded in dutiful agreement with whatever Silliman might have
said in that day's blog posting. I was disturbed that the diarylike qualities
of the blog could seamlessly transform into a venue for poetry's celebrity
culture—celebrating the authority of Silliman, the poet and poetry critic,
even when he's writing at length on Hollywood blockbusters or reality
TV shows like *Project Runway*—rather than function as a space for the
creation of new writing. I decided Shimmy needed an extended, regularly
updated blog, and her blog needed to be a performance venue as well as
a journal—a place where new work can be invented, tinkered with, and
showcased. This would be a site to channel Shimmy's rage, to practice
appropriation, and to find new spaces for writerly experimentation while
still chronicling my life (shimmykat.blogspot.com).

"Chronicling his life" . . . through his cat? He *has* to be one of *those*
writers. To some extent, maybe; perhaps it's more a question of what parts
of my life I am chronicling.

For instance, Shimmy's blog finally gave me a chance to use the photographs of cattle I had taken in 2004 at the home next door to Donald
Rumsfeld's in Taos. But as I translated Shimmy's feelings about Rumsfeld—yes, I talk this way, staying in character as the blog's performative
translator rather than as mere diarist—it was clear that a serial narrative
was emerging.

"Faces and horns, anonymous bodies, the cattle who live next door
to Rumsfeld's home in Taos burst into our apartment," I translated.
"Flies buzzed their rumps." The cattle were no longer anonymous animals living next door to the then secretary of defense. Instead, they were
trying to escape Rumsfeld, as much of the world seemed to be doing in
late 2005: "They were running from the Secretary of Defense, fleeing
another of his blood ritual masses at the manse in Taos (a Chevy Chev-
elle sits on blocks in the tall grass next door) where he camped as a Boy
Scout in 1948."

As often is the case with Shimmy's blog, where villains try to charm
their way into her prose, Rumsfeld attempted to enchant her: "'Shimmy,
come sit on my lap.'" It was Rumsfeld, old and plump, tapping his fingers on the arm of the sofa, mimicking the doomed pitter-patter of mice.

"'Don't be afraid of me. Look at all these cattle! I'm friends with the animals.'"

Shimmy eventually spoke back to Rumsfeld in language appropriated from the texts of Situationist Raoul Vaneigem. Of course, in Shimmy's world, all Rumsfeld could do was speak in appropriations of the tortured rhetoric to which the rest of us had grown accustomed during his televised press conferences. "I'm not into this detail stuff," he said to her, "I'm more concepty."

"Y Tu Rumsfeld Tambien" was a serial narrative, but entries in Shimmy's Blog are also opportunities to experiment with nonlinear composition. Whether working with narrative or nonlinearity, I use Shimmy's blog as a way to hone the postmodern appropriative techniques that have a large influence on my poems.

During the composition of another poem for *Historic Diary,* I experimented with a piece comprised entirely of questions asked in the original film version of *The Manchurian Candidate.* I didn't quite know what form the poem was taking yet. As I would in a traditional spiral-bound journal, I began jotting questions asked in the film into the blog; and as I did this, the questions themselves started to suggest patterns of formal fragmentation and narrative erasure that told a kind of story:

What's the matter with her? Hey, Shimmy, what about my robe? What's your personal advice? May I take this thing off now, Shimmy? How many Communists did you say? Can you see the red queen? You will be taken for a checkup—is that clear? What's your last name? What's your last name? The letter? Have you got the letter? What sort of greeting is that at 3:30 in the morning? Are you sure they're coming to the party, Shimmy? Are you absolutely sure? What are you supposed to be, one of those Dutch skaters? Why don't we just sneak away for a few minutes and sit down somewhere quietly and stare out the window? Shimmy, why don't you pass the time by playing a little solitaire? Aren't you going to pop champagne, or dance in the streets, or at least slide your food dish around the kitchen floor? Fifty-two red queens and I are telling you—you know what we're telling you?

It was crucial for me to see these appropriated questions from the film recast in a bounded journal-like space of my own—that is, in the blog.

After I wrote this posting, the repetitious nature of the questions suggested the pantoum form. As I drafted and revised this emerging pantoum in my word-processing program, the blog posting eventually helped me create the poem's three penultimate stanzas:

> Can you see the red queen?
> Where are you, Raymond?
> Raymond, do you remember murdering Mavole and Lembeck?
> Fifty-two red queens and me are telling you—do you know what
>   we're telling you?
> Where are you, Raymond?
> They can make me do anything, Ben, can't they?
> Fifty-two red queens and me are telling you—do you know what
>   we're telling you?
> Ben, you don't blame me for hating my mother, do you?
> "The Queen of Diamonds?" What did she mean, "The Queen of
>   Diamonds?"
> May I have the bayonet, please?
> Have you ever killed anyone?
> Do you know what we're telling you?

The creepy, predatory pitch of Angela Lansbury's voice reflected in the blog posting ("Can you see the red queen? . . . You will be taken for a checkup—is that clear?") became a model for the poem's tone. The poem was initially conceived and rehearsed in my "notebook," as if Shimmy's blog were a spiral-bound journal for first drafts. Without such rehearsal, much of the formal and tonal nuances of the poem might be lost.

I didn't realize it, but my initial desire to create Shimmy's blog as a parodic intervention into the blogosphere had transformed itself, instead, into an extension of my lifelong journaling. Blogging provides an audience for an artist's untamed journal drafts. But given the medium of blogging, its existence within the extensive and searchable interconnections of the World Wide Web, a blog also offers the writer a performative space—a venue that combines the childlike (or in this case, the child-arsonistlike) wild-zone of invention with the immediate responsiveness of an audience. Shimmy's blog stretches me, as a writer, beyond the limits of journaling or letter writing, because a blog, after all, can be simultaneously a diary and a piece of performance art.

Indeed, Shimmy reviews movies—an unusual practice for a private journal but appropriate for a blog, like hers, that is part-diary and part-performance. Because Shimmy is a housecat, her movie reviews necessarily function as both conceptual art pieces and journaling exercises. Her reviews are simply readings of what is happening in the apartment while Shelly and I are at the theater.

Shimmy's reviews are an extension of my own love-hate obsessions with popular culture in my poems—as in my new manuscript, where Soviet and U.S. popular culture embed themselves whenever possible in Lee Harvey Oswald's myths and texts. The blog also reflects the pop-culture influence of my editorial work as one of the founders and editors of *Court Green,* a poetry journal that has devoted special sections in past issues to film and political poems; every issue publishes a number of poems influenced by popular culture and new media.

Shimmy's child-arsonist blog persona is for me an invigorating extension of the creative process wild-zone that journaling and letter writing give us permission to indulge in. And best of all, the blog functions in an arena that overlaps the traditional diary and traditional letter / e-mail. It has been convenient for me to discuss in utilitarian terms the correlation between Shimmy's blog and my poems. To use the phrase *child vandal,* as I do earlier in this essay to describe my revisionary attitude toward the Warren Commission is, of course, to suggest *child- arsonist* and, by extension, could be an effort to persuade you that I am not one of *those* writers—especially one of those poets who identifies too much with the cats of this world. Using the phrase *child vandal* suggests that I am writing only about my art form, about Shimmy's Blog as mere utilitarian tributary into the larger stream. To do otherwise would be to presume, yikes, that I *would* want to chronicle my life through my cat.

I do protest too much, don't I? I'm thinking of something James Broughton once wrote: "It is better to live poetically than to write good poems." I found this quotation in his archives while working in Special Collections; as far as I know, it's not published anywhere. I tried to include it as an epigraph for the literary magazine I was editing at the time. But my fellow editorial board members hesitated. I don't blame them, because they, like me, were worried that the quotation might be true. Were we living poetically? We certainly were trying like mad to write good poems. But was Broughton right? And if he was correct, then our greatest ideal, to live poetically and write good poems, might be a loss. At the time, I was a heavy notebook journaler, and for me the journal was a space for intense living and writing—it was the space for diary entries, for working out emotional conundrums, for transcribing memorable quotations, for jotting down poem drafts and fragments, for cutting out relevant newspaper articles. It was part daybook and part creative-writing logbook. As such, it was the space where I really was testing whether I could both live poetically and write good poems.

Shimmy's blog serves much the same purpose for me, extending performatively those original daybooks. I still don't know how to integrate the spirit of Broughton's statement in my life. I probably won't ever know if I've accomplished this. When I talk about the quotation with other writers, most feel the need to make some kind of peace with it, too. The blogosphere is for me a space where the rough drafts of my everyday lived experience and of my everyday writing projects can live on top of each other like palimpsests, a space where the writing of a film review, and by extension, the writing of poem drafts and all other modes of journaling and performing, can occur simultaneously with the quotidian happenings of my life.

The blog is the place where the personal and the historical collide—where everyday lived experience exists conterminously with the historical imagination. Lately in my poetry, I've been trying to fuse the personal and the historical, so that the poems perform a particular selfhood without succumbing to self-obsession. Shimmy's blog offers a public venue for me to rehearse this complication of selfhood in my writing. The blog is circumscribed by a persona and by nontransparent forms of language that "ghost" the world rather than render it as something whole or self-contained.

Part 2

THE JOURNAL FOR SURVIVAL

Life can only be understood backwards, but it must be lived forward.

Søren Kierkegaard, quoted in Howard V. Horg, *The Essential Kierkegaard* (2000)

"MUSEMENTS" AND
MENTAL HEALTH

Zan Bockes

Thirty-six years and one hundred thirty-five spiral notebooks ago, my daily journal was born of an innate desire to set down the thoughts, feelings, and events that shaped me. Written with a watery blue fountain pen, the initial yellow, seventy-sheet notebook was jammed with the antics of a thirteen-year-old girl. Since then, my transformation from silly, egotistical teenager to seasoned adult has been fully documented, including the development of my mental illness.

I was diagnosed with bipolar disorder (manic depression) when I was nineteen, and it has affected me in profound ways. Years of swinging through the revolving door of mania, depression, and psychosis have left me with a trail of mental health hospitalizations and treatments.

To deal with my illness, I turned to writing as a therapeutic measure, as it soothes me and serves as a crucial coping mechanism. I feel a sense of catharsis as I try to capture the flood of ideas and overwhelming emotions. Conversing with another person never allows the same coherence I can reach when I read over written sentences. I am talking to myself on paper, able to follow the threads more effectively because they are registered in ink. I've come to appreciate these states a little more, and journaling has enabled me to articulate what I've learned, and given me the ability to convey them in my more public fiction and poetry. Needless to say, I've gathered plenty of material.

At an early age, I cultivated a close friendship with pen and paper that has long been central to my life. I've always considered myself a writer, mainly because I make a habit of scribbling things down. I gain a sensual pleasure from the loops and curls of the cursive hand flowing from my mind to an open page and how the complexities of language surface from the curve and tangle of lines.

For me, the words these images form are forever sacred, the most powerful tools created.

When I learned to write at age five, the main audience for my nascent creations was my parents. Long before I could spell, my stories about our family were written phonetically, as my father taught me, each word sounded out with exquisite care. I recently stumbled upon one of those carefully bound "chapbooks," giving directions for making "feeshing powalls" out of a stick and a "peass of streang." Rough illustrations of fishing poles clarify the process to aid the reader in deciphering the clumsy letters and abominable spelling.

I kept sporadic notes in first grade, mostly reporting the weather. I'd already developed a compulsion to record things, and my first attempts at journaling were superficial, having to do with daily routines and the occasional sentence about some less-than-usual activity. My father gave me a five-year diary with a lock and key, and I wrote diligently every day on the three little lines allotted. After a while, I became impatient with the cramped spaces and began to fill the entire page, defying the whole tradition and tossing the five-year format to the wind.

These days, I keep four notebooks. The first is my continuing daily account of emotions and thoughts, events, and insights. Another holds my first drafts of prose and poetry. A third is a pocket-sized notepad for ideas, lines, and titles that come to me at stray moments. The fourth contains an experimental venture—a form which I call musements.

Musements are similar to prose poems, in that they look like a block of prose, but taste like poetry. Every day I spend five minutes writing continuously, and the results (completely unrevised) serve as a jump-start for my morning writing routine. I think of them as a sort of literary mandala, meditatively capturing the whimsies of my subconscious. They begin with a title, and what follows is completely unpredictable. Here's an example from January 9, 2007:

Placebo Panacea

The pill I swallow, distilled by light, haloes my brain with happiness and the distant refrain of a song I love but cannot remember. Each morning, the bell twines its tones through my ears and clears my head with a small buzz of delight. Everyone should take such medicine—the dose that pulls you close to death, then sets you free, vision catapulted to wild image, your mind living the dance on the offhand chance a miracle will happen today. Gratitude is the tune I like—a slight jingle, like magic flashing in a hand, like coins in the pocket of a man whose life is blissfully easy.

The musements and their carefree nature loosen up my mind and hand, and occasionally they have stimulated more focused poems and fiction. Some have appeared in small literary magazines. At the very least, they are fun to compose—my basic requirement for any creative endeavor.

As a teenager, I was relieved to discover the verbal freedom of a more-or-less private notebook. Through the business of setting down the daily minutiae, I understood the value in telling the truth. Because I had to be painfully sincere about what I thought and felt, I developed a better rapport with the writer and primary reader—myself. I gained a clearer sense of my own voice by practicing on paper and hearing myself speak as I wrote down each word. But I could also speak on others' behalf, and I thought it a refreshing exercise to tell about my day from the viewpoint of my brother or a friend. This helped my later attempts at dialogue and stories inspired by other perspectives.

But my mother often snooped through my bedroom and read my notebook if it were left out. I could tell, because she dislodged the items I'd carefully placed on it to signal unlawful entry. The pencil I'd put on top was now off to the side, or I'd lined up the cover with the edge of the desk and now it had moved over by an inch. I never accused her, and she said nothing to me either, probably not wanting to confess she'd been invading my privacy.

I was horrified that my own mother could not be trusted to respect my personal space. At first I was angry, until I realized it was a marvelous opportunity to practice my skill at lying. I began keeping another log for her perusal, regaling my fictional experiences with sex and illicit drugs. Some days she approached me with caution and deep concern, and I secretly gloated, knowing she'd peeked at the fake journal. For a few months I kept two diaries—the true one for myself (which I hid in the back of my closet) and the false one for my mother. Every evening, I continued the duplicity, first entering the day's less interesting events, and then exercising my imagination for my mother's benefit. Maintaining my conversational style for her entertainment was a unique challenge—how could I tell about my twenty-three-year-old boyfriend without revealing I'd made him up? Although I thoroughly enjoyed myself for a while, all this writing took up precious time, and when my grades began to suffer, I abandoned the project.

At first, I addressed the "real" wire-bound tablets to "Dear Friend." I had no concrete idea who this friend was, but it seemed helpful to imagine an interested audience. I realized that I was not writing for myself, as the act of registering anything guarantees the chance that another's eyes will see it. Hopefully those eyes will appreciate its content and quality, a wish that I initially harbored, but as the years have passed I've grown far less concerned about this vague audience's approval. An almost brutal honesty has arisen, uncomplicated by the apprehension that some future reader will dislike whatever is revealed. Now, I just don't care, preferring to concentrate on integrity and on understanding my place in the psychiatric system.

As I try to help myself recover from my symptoms, I pay particular attention to my experience at the time. At points when my mental health is shaky, journaling serves as a means for overcoming the onslaught of suffering. In October of 2006, I struggled through a tumultuous episode of mania and psychosis, during which I was confined in a "crisis house" for more than two weeks. The two journal entries below are examples of my state of mind.

October 2, 2006

Man, I wish this would go away and I could get better. Shaking, zinging, repeating, echoing, lips moving constantly to the dance of the thoughts and voices in my head.

Gotta Normalize NOW! Starting now, starting now, starting now . . . SHIT!

I cannot imagine my normal life right now—just working, writing, checking email, going to the health club—cannot imagine it.

The next day's entry continues to describe my episode.

October 3, 2006

I've been telling myself this will be an okay day, but I've been unable to convince myself.

Zipping, zinging, nervous, shaking, my voice and others in my head repeating, repeating, repeating.

I don't know what to do about this. After over a week and a half,
I'm no better than I was when this started.

But I AM better—I must be. The staff here has noticed improve-
ment, even though I can't see it myself. I'm talking softer to myself.
I pace and rock less. But still I get shivers of fear.

From my first psychiatric hospitalization in 1980 onward, my note-
taking was often remarked upon by the nurses and physicians who treated
me. In my medical chart, they called it hypergraphia, a term defining my
relentless push to get everything down. I had to write. I wanted only to
put some semblance of order to the chaos, stave off my fears of disinte-
gration. The writing helped me focus and communicate.

But the hospital staff discouraged my "writing behavior" because, as
they said, it interfered with my "process of socialization." I was not per-
mitted to have my usual spiral notebook, as it posed a security threat—
patients could decapitate themselves with the wire binding—so I had to
make do with pieces of scrap paper and a stubby pencil. I wrote furiously,
nearly oblivious to my surroundings, but desperately needing the oblivion. Unfortunately, my efforts to calm myself and concentrate more on
the realities of my situation were dismissed as symptoms of my illness.

Even more distressing were the medications I was required to take.
Most of them deadened my mind and spirit, and I wrote little, ignoring
my journal for weeks at a time. Simply, I had nothing to say—nothing
sparked my interest enough to bother describing it. The poverty of the
few entries during these periods says it all. In addition, side effects such
as restlessness, drooling, heavy sedation, and weight gain persuaded me to
abandon the drugs again and again, which only seemed to exacerbate my
symptoms. At times, the "cure" was worse than the illness.

In the hospital, the staff snooped through my notes, like my prying
mother. Often they discarded them without my permission, ignoring
them as "ravings" instead of an essential component of my treatment. My
insistence on their necessity was merely further indication of my ill state.

The negative response from my caregivers escalated my frustration. At
the least, we had conflicting perceptions of what was helpful and what
was not. As a psychiatric patient, I had no credibility whatsoever; everything I said and did was suspect. When I claimed that writing helped me,
I was confronted with rolling eyes and scoffs of disbelief. However,
there were a few nurses who listened to my protests. They supported my
need for written expression and even went so far as to give me some

quiet time each day for my literary pursuits. With gratitude, I still remember those nurses.

Occasionally I'll spend some time randomly reading older journal entries. I'm always surprised by what I've forgotten and what I've repressed and even shocked by parallels and chagrined by blatant foolishness. Often I get downright bored and skip over large portions. It's Reality TV without the relief of commercial breaks and editors.

I believe that if I spent more time rereading, I would discover some refreshing insights. I do not reread often, and I don't quite understand my reluctance. I must be currently blind to patterns and histories that I am afraid to explore. Maybe too much honesty is presently unbearable, and I do not wish to see my mistakes and pettiness exposed.

Yet, I see myself clearly with every line, with my faults and strengths, guilt and regrets. Perhaps I still need a way to define myself and my world as a narcissistic defense against mortality and meaninglessness. I used to crave being "special," which required asserting my originality in whatever way I could. The act of recounting my life seemed to instill it with purpose, giving me a sense that I could live forever, or as long as my journal escaped decay. The fact that I still write daily may only mean that I continue to delude myself that I am important, my existence worthy of print.

But rereading can have another purpose: The sheer wealth of material never fails to produce stories and ideas. Descriptions of landscapes and settings evoke a sense of place—I have written of the mountains outside my kitchen window here in Missoula, Montana; the majesty of thunderstorms in Omaha, Nebraska, where I was raised; and the people in the street below my room at the Boston YMCA.

Story plots arise from half-remembered incidents. A babysitting job turns into a nightmare when the parents come home early. A woman steals a police car. A runaway teenager sells her grandmother's diamond ring.

Composites of characters emerge—my mother's lilting voice, with her preference for aphorisms, speaks from an eighty-year-old woman's mouth (the lips ringed with small wrinkles) about a dead son who had my brother's tendency to laugh in his sleep and my first boyfriend's habit of answering a question with a question. I see no end to the possibilities presented by a thorough journal, or by the regular composition of the mind-liberating musements.

I've prescribed the art of creating musements for a fellow poet who lacks self-confidence, resulting in an extended hiatus in her literary work.

But the daily habit of forcing her hand to write has, over time, helped her capture the undertones of despair that have hindered her creativity. The musements gave rise to a freer and less self-conscious expression, and now she produces poetry at a level she was previously unable to attain.

I've also encouraged a few friends to keep journals. My brother, who suffers from depression, has remarked that reading back over his daily accounts has enabled him to see patterns of which he was once unaware. He's gained insights and ideas for keeping himself healthy, and now has the company of a receptive self when he finds himself sliding back down.

A good friend who recently lost her husband has turned to writing when her grief was most acute. In the form of letters to him, she relives the best moments they had together and the things she misses about him. She's found the writing therapeutic, and as a tribute she is collecting a scrapbook of memories.

I am pleased that these other writers have found comfort in the same medium that has engaged me for so many years. My journal remains my closest and most consistent companion, an endless source of informa- tion and inspiration and a detailed account of my journey. It has seen me through tumultuous times, enhanced my honesty with myself and my understanding of pain. Basically, I survive to write because I write to survive.

When I was thirteen, I had no way of knowing that the first spiral notebook would beget one hundred and thirty-four more. Or that I'd enjoy such a loving relationship with that blue fountain pen and lined paper. Or that the original "Dear Friend" would evolve into the woman I know today.

Life has a lovely way of being capricious and unpredictable—some- what like a musement—and for me, journaling has restored meaning to the journey. I believe that, in a sense, my writing justifies my existence, even if my eyes are the only ones to appreciate it. At the base of it all remains my love of words—their comfort, their power, their sanctity.

CLEARING
THE DECKS

Kathleen Gerard

It was a simple spiral notebook. On the front cover was scrawled R-E-A-D in tall, capital letters. The word was encased in a big circle that had a diagonal slash running through it. I had seen my sister—older than I by four years—regularly curled up on the bed across from mine in the room we shared, spilling ink on the pages of that book, sometimes for hours on end. *What in the world is she writing about in there?* Although I was only thirteen, I respected my sister and wouldn't dare invade her privacy. But more to the fact, I knew she was crackerjack smart and ingenious, and I suspected that she had probably booby-trapped the book in some way as a safeguard against temptation. Coupled with that was the fine print I'd once seen centered beneath her blatant do-not-read symbol: *If you're close enough to read this, put down my journal right NOW, and get a life of your own to write about!*

I heeded the warning and went no further.

A year later, I would discover a life of my own to write about, when my father, at the age of forty-five, died of a sudden and massive heart attack. The safe and sheltered world I'd taken for granted suddenly tilted on its axis. There was the wake, the funeral, and the repast. But once the generous outpourings of sympathy and condolences evaporated, and I resumed my life as a high school sophomore, an undercurrent of discontent and loneliness began to swell within me.

I longed to return to the old routine—for things to go back to normal. But *normal* was no more. Listening to my friends obsess over their hair and boys and what they'd wear to the Snowball Dance made me feel out of sync. Did any of that really matter if you could, one night, right after watching *Saturday Night Live*, feel a touch of *agita* in your chest and minutes later, poof—you took your last breath and were gone?

I had always been shy, sensitive, and self-contained. But I profoundly missed my father, and I wanted—and needed—to talk about him and what had happened. My friends, however, weren't receptive to such laments. They wanted the old Kathy back—the one who was fun and focused on things that fourteen-year-old girls were supposed to focus on. But I couldn't. I no longer perceived the world in the same way as my peers, and they didn't understand. How could they? My father's passing had created a chasm—a widening moat—that distanced me from people, while at the same time it also spurred the development of a rich, complex inner life.

At any other time, I would have confided in my mother—she was my touchstone—but she was struggling to manage her own grief and a full-time job. Because she seemed so vulnerable, I was also terrified that, if I burdened her, she might succumb to the same fate as my father. And my sister? Well, she was back at college, hours away. I figured I had two choices. I could either let the chasm isolate me to the point that I'd be swallowed up, or I could try to build a bridge and get across it. It was that realization—and the grace of God—that finally encouraged me to stop at the stationery store and purchase a notebook similar to the ones I'd seen my sister rely on all those years. Staring at the blank page of my very first journal, I took a deep breath, set my pen upon the paper, and wrote a letter to my father—more like a prayer—asking that he intercede for me and help me get through.

"Writing a journal means that facing your ocean, you are afraid to swim across it," wrote George Sand, "so you attempt to drink it drop by drop." My early efforts at keeping a journal were sporadic, and what I conveyed was rather repetitive. But that was the beauty of it—there were no rules. I simply opened the book and wrote down whatever came to mind. That included snippets of things that happened at school or at home; conversations or conflicts; my fears; things I'd witnessed or read, mostly quotes and lines from poems or song lyrics that spoke to me. My journal became a safe place where my voice and my feelings could finally be heard, and my perceptions counted. It was in using my journal to filter out stress and strife that I suddenly felt more hopeful and empowered. I deduced that if I compartmentalized the disconnect of my grief—

transposed all that was troubling me onto the pages of my journal—I could keep afloat, and in the process, I could propel myself forward across the chasm. I knew I could never return to the same world of which I was once a part, but I could navigate my voyage to a new world—one full of self-understanding and realization, as well as knowledge.

Thus, my liberation began and has since become a regular, daily habit that I have practiced for more than twenty-five years. It is in keeping a journal—starting an entry and finishing it, usually in twenty-minute increments—that I eventually uncover how the events of my life unfold, and I open a door to gain access to my feelings. When visual artists talk about "training the eye," they generally mean honing a sense of instinct, learning to see the relationships among colors and objects; form and space. It's about perception. Keeping a journal does that, too. It is a way of teaching yourself to look more closely at the world in order to better inform your life and your work—especially if you're a storyteller. For me, it is by committing the events of my life to the page that I can explore and sort through my feelings via organic, stream-of-consciousness writing. I focus on whatever comes to mind—for as long as I care to look and as deep as I dare to delve. I begin to see connections between events. I retrieve abandoned truths about myself and other people, and the world and my place in it. In the end, stories are born, and often I'm enlightened to the point of epiphany. As the poet and essayist Henry David Thoreau wrote in his journal in 1851, "The question is not what you look at, but what you see." He may have been speaking about nature, but it is also the nature of all creating, especially writing.

I didn't know it at the time, but my early reliance on a journal helped me practice how to be a writer and became the impetus for me later to answer the call to make writing and storytelling the focus of my life. Over the years, what started out as a way to maintain a connection to my father has evolved. These days, I find that I write less to him in my journal and more to a force within myself, a higher power. In the process of keeping journals—reviewing and mining them for material from time to time (mostly referring to the emotional subtext underlying events and experiences)—I've come to appreciate the lessons of my life. I can rediscover and more deeply understand the person I was, the person I am, and the person I aspire to become—and why. I can track how I've gotten from there to here; how I've dealt with experiences in the past, which can help shape my present, and, I hope, provide insight to guide my future.

Keeping a journal has also helped me pay closer attention to life as it unfolds, and it has taught me how to live. Because of this, everything that happens to me, great or small, can become potential fodder for my work as a professional writer. Hence, my journal becomes a laboratory which explores happenings that can range from the mundane to the sublime to the philosophical: how one of my friends stood me up at the gym; struggling to pull together an essay to meet a deadline; the escalating threat of violence in the world; my glee at having no cavities at the dentist; how I can't stop thinking that maybe the phrase I saw—"There is no finish line"—printed on the back of a jogger's T-shirt, might have an underlying personal message for me; and my abiding fears about how I might succumb to a recurrence of cancer one day.

Taking mental note of so many experiences and influences—positive and negative—can serve as inspiration. However, if too many things pile up and press on my psyche, distraction and a lack of focus can result. That's where my journal repeatedly comes into play. I start every day with at least *twenty minutes at the book,* as I call it—although sometimes twenty minutes can extend to hours. When I open the book—a $2.49 college-ruled Steno pad—it transforms into a combination of trusted friend, therapist, and spiritual advisor. By writing about whatever comes to mind, I'm able to synthesize thought and feeling. And by bridging my outer and inner worlds and reflecting upon the intersection of the two, I am better able to achieve emotional, psychic, and spiritual wholeness. Thus, my journal becomes a form of written meditation—where I let go of all inhibition until what's important is sifted from what is not. In essence, I purge some of the emotional clutter piling up inside of me until I finally clear the decks enough to illuminate my soul. This sense of clarity lightens the load and better enables me to get my professional writing done. And I've found that the more disciplined I am in keeping that twenty-minute ritual, the more I am able to tap into my creativity and get my prose under control.

For example, when I was thirty-four-years old, I awoke to find a lump under my arm. In the process of having a biopsy and learning I had cancer, I traipsed from one medical doctor to the next—waiting sometimes weeks between appointments. Deeply shaken, fear gripped me in paralyzing proportions. I was rattled to the core. As a structured person, I knew the best way to keep afloat and stay productive was to continue to commit daily to my journal—no matter what. But with things in such a state of flux, there were many days when I just didn't want to write at all. I didn't feel like facing the truth and grappling with my feelings. I longed to escape. So I made a bargain with myself: *Do your twenty minutes, then the rest of the day is yours. At least you'll keep your writing muscles from atrophy.* With that in mind, I decided that because I was so emotional and unsettled, I'd use my journal simply to document factual events as they were happening—whether medical consultations or where I met friends for lunch. Deep down, I trusted the process, believing that the sense of disciplined constancy—however modified—could anchor me through the arising challenges. That left weeks of mere record keeping as one would write in a diary. But by showing up for those twenty minutes and sticking to the facts, my emotions gradually began to rise to the surface and they slowly started to color each entry. Here is an excerpt from one of my journal breakthroughs:

Met X at the Iron Horse for lunch yesterday. Crowded. Waited long for a table. Menu so extensive, I couldn't decide what the heck I wanted. Why do there have to be so many choices? My mind is a jumble and patience is running thin these days. Settled on the tried and true—a salad. X joined me . . . X is up to her eyeballs in wedding plans. She's really beaming. I'm truly happy that's she's so happy, but it was hard for me to get psyched for her when so much is preying on me. I didn't want to rain on her parade, so I kept firing off questions and got her talking about herself. I'm good at that, and I think listening to her go on and on—about gowns, flowers, banquet halls, menus, invitations and music—was a perfect antidote for me. It served as a distraction—at least for while. When I went to the ladies' room and looked in the mirror, I felt like maybe none of this was real. Maybe the cancer diagnosis happened to someone else. Maybe I've just been dreaming. But somehow, over the course of our nibbling on spinach salads, when the conversation veered to me, the realness of it hit me again. I began to relay to X some of the details of what the last specialist told me . . . When X simply nodded in response—silent and not offering any sort of verbal comment or opinion—I felt heat rise in my face and neck. Perspiring hot, I was nervous and scared by her response—or lack thereof. Was I boring her? Sounding repetitive? Was it that she didn't know what to say? Or was I reading into things too much—letting my over-active imagination run roughshod? Maybe it had nothing at all to do with the cancer? Maybe it had only to do with X being afraid to open her mouth for fear that some of that spinach salad might be wedged in her front teeth?

That rambling paragraph, written in stream-of-consciousness style in my journal, later became the seed for a short story called "The Undertaking" that I wrote over the course of my cancer odyssey. In rereading the journal entry, I found that spewing the details of that lunch onto the pages of my journal had underlying story potential. The last sentence, about the spinach salad, even triggered me to laugh. Thus, I decided to go the next step. Why not open a portal into my imagination and give myself carte blanche, recreating the emotional subtext of that journal entry into a fictional event? I started with the spinach salad and the wedding plans. I skewed the variables and channeled them through a prism of absurdity, trying to build a story around them. When I finally juxtaposed the whole idea of a wedding against my fears about pain, suffering, and even the prospect of death, my apprehension and anxiety began to diffuse, and I even started to entertain myself. Through months of writes and rewrites, "The Undertaking" eventually evolved into a short story about a woman whose fiancé dumps her, and in the throes of hopelessness and despondency, she convinces herself that she will never have a wedding of her own. Therefore, she undertakes to preplan her funeral with as much pizzazz as she would her wedding. In the end, she even gives her wake and repast a dress rehearsal and births herself into a brand new life.

In writing the story, I primarily lifted that passage from my journal and let it incubate until it mutated into something much larger. Here is how things finally boiled down and were shaped into the final draft that appeared in *Writers' Forum* in the winter of 2001:

> She cringed at the thought of being alone . . . Oh, such an impoverished, interminable fate. And she imagined herself turning to friends over lunch, those who would nod politely at her harangues over her life's unfairness while they nibbled on spinach salad—concerned that one of those dark, leafy greens would get wedged in their front teeth—acting as if they were listening at the same time.

This story (which was later adapted and produced as an off-Broadway play) became the gift of my illness, all because of one simple paragraph that took root on the pages of my journal. In following and exploring my feelings via the writing process, my cancer (and the forces surrounding it) became like a grain of sand trapped inside an oyster shell. By showing up and keeping my commitment each day, I not only mustered the courage to stay connected to myself and the situation, but ultimately I sparked my imagination and energized my enthusiasm. It was by churning and gritting against the grain of sand that my writing—in both my journal and in the short story—worked together to encompass the full range of my emotions and creativity. The end result—a pearl!

Writing is an act of faith, and words are a powerful force—my sister's warning, the letter I wrote to my father, how writing in my journal can serve as a launch pad for other work. Most people barely have time to live their lives, let alone sit down and ponder their existence on the page. But I believe that especially for a writer, your home is your soul, and it's hard to comfortably inhabit a place filled with too much clutter. That is why, as a staple of my daily diet, like brushing my teeth and taking my vitamins—I make it my mission each day to depend upon those *twenty minutes with the book*. Staring at the blank page, I never know what shape things will take or if what I write will have story potential. All I know and surrender to is the familiar sense of relief and healing that comes from clearing the decks and putting my house in order day after day after day.

LE MISÉRABLE

Maureen Stanton

M y journals are a compendium of my misery. I said this to my friend Nancy one night, and she was inspired to write a song. I said, "I'm glad my suffering is a source for your creative impulse." If anyone were to read my journals, they'd find me depressive, obsessive, pessimistic, narcissistic, self-pitying, and dull. When I'm happy, I rarely write in my journals, hence their one-sidedness. When I'm happy, sometimes I reread my journals to visit my misery, and I like to do that because it helps me appreciate my fleeting happiness even more. It's also true that when I am sad and compelled to record my despair, I reread my laments recorded on previous days and find they have an unnerving similarity. This visitation to my past is instructive—my own hand warning me about ruts in my thinking and unhealthy patterns in my life—but it is also oddly comforting. Misery loves company, even its own. My misery loves my misery.

Virginia Woolf reread her journal notes:

"I got out this diary and read, as one always does read one's own writing, with a kind of guilty intensity," she writes in her diary, which has a weird insular quality, a conversation with one's self, one's past. "I confess that the rough and random style of it, often so ungrammatical, and crying for a word altered, afflicted me somewhat. I am trying to tell whichever self it is that reads this hereafter that I can write very much better."

Whichever self. I find it hopeful that she imagined a future self, or several possible selves, to whom she was writing. Imagining a future self is imagining a future.

I've written in a diary or journal since my childhood days, although I don't have most of these volumes anymore. My diary from 1970 was yellow with a bird on the cover and had faint, blue-lined pages. There were few entries, although I bothered to pencil in "Nothing Interesting" for days on end, so often that I eventually took to jotting simply "N.I." on each page. But one summer day the year I turned ten, I went raspberry picking down by the train tracks at the end of our dead-end street, and was so excited by the size of one berry that I drew a replica of it in my journal. Even now I remember exaggerating the size as I sketched the fruit. (I must have eaten the berry, so had no model for my illustration.) I was so excited by this luscious berry, like a found treasure, that I was compelled to record it for posterity. Even now, nearly forty years later, it makes me happy to read about this raspberry; I delight now in my delight then, as in the famous line by the prolific diarist Anaïs Nin—"We write to taste life twice, in the moment and in reflection."

When I was twenty-eight, my mother sold the house in which I grew up and had left a decade earlier. Before she closed the deal, she presented me with a box of artifacts from my life—some college textbooks, photo albums, and a small red diary with a gold lock. I hadn't known the diary existed. I did not remember keeping the diary in 1975 when I was fifteen. Although I could *imagine* myself lying on my bed with the lime green bedspread with my door locked, hunched over the tiny diary, I could not remember a single moment doing this. The truth is that I don't remember much from those few years between the ages of fifteen and eighteen, when I strayed from my straight and narrow path as the captain of the cheerleading squad and the basketball team, to a more crooked trail— drug addiction and juvenile delinquency.

The diary began at the end of ninth grade, at the start of this sad transition, my fall from grace (the first, I suppose). At twenty-eight, when my mother gave me the diary, I couldn't wait to get a chunk of time to crawl into my past, reenter 1975, and see who I was in that inchoate stage. I was nervous and excited, understanding that a year of my life that had been lost might be returned to me, and that I might discover something about myself then, that would help me know myself better now.

My first reaction was one of disappointment, even embarrassment. For weeks, every page was consumed by the activities of Dennis Tetreault and whether or not I saw him in the halls of West Junior High. Surely if I bothered to write, surely if I tarried with pen and paper, I would have more to say than, "I love Dennis and I hate Beth. I know she is after him. Lisa Higgins is a flirt and an asshole." I eventually forgave myself for a lack of gravitas in adolescence, but what made me weep after I finished reading this diary was the senseless and wasteful self-destruction that marked my sophomore year, when it was clear that I didn't know or love myself at all.

Here is an excerpt.

Saturday, December 20, 1975

Walked downtown and saw Boomer, Mike Guisti and Bob Taylor. They drove us on a couple dust runs. I got pretty dusted. Went up to Guisti's house after. Lisa puked her guts out. Bob Taylor turned me on to some fantastic hits. Got very blown and had to go home. Good thing Ma wasn't up when I got in. Everything I saw was double. Wish I didn't have to come home at all.

"Dusted" refers to the altered state after one smokes angel dust (PCP), which I did every day for about a year. Reading these entries—in my rounded girlish penmanship—was painful. Now thinking about that period is painful. There must have been some happiness, something redemptive, because, after all, I lived, or chose to (I recall thinking back then about not living). Or maybe back then subconsciously I wrote in hopes of a future self.

In my junior year of high school, I graduated from those small bound diaries with their predetermined, equal allotments of space for each day, to spiral-bound notebooks. I wrote during class—flunking geometry, which was an otherwise easy subject made hopelessly boring by Mrs. Drane, and I was often stoned in class. My mother told me she'd thrown those journals away after she'd found them underneath my mattress one day, because she was disgusted by what she'd read. I wish I still had those notebooks so I could know myself better, understand how I turned my life around, quit drugs, made it to college (in spite of thirty-five absences and fourteen tardies that year), and began to recognize myself. Perhaps writing in those journals helped to save me, transferred the story to a place outside myself, my body, where I could look at it plainly and then leave it behind.

Now that I understand how I mostly turn to journals when feeling despair, fear, anxiety, depression, loneliness, and understand how happy moments are largely unrecorded, perhaps I can project backward onto those teenage years some joy that wasn't noted, that I was then the same sort of diarist I am now: one-sided.

The difference between a journal and a diary can be detected in the etymology. The Latin root of diary is *diarium,* which means daily allowance. Diaries are more external, I think, recording events of the day, what one did with one's time in the sixteen or so hours of wakefulness, our daily allowance of life. Diaries record events, like Samuel Pepys's volumes, written over the course of nine years. They recount everyday life—the minor events (a night at an auction), and the major events (the great fire of London and the plague). A diary is a daily accounting, a listing of items, such as Thoreau's estimates of the cost of food for eight months, like molasses ($1.73) and rice ($1.73 ½). Or the size of a raspberry. Or a list of drugs consumed.

The Latin word for journal, *diurnus,* shares the same root, but with an important distinction; it means "of the day, journey." A journal takes you places, like a captain's log, even if those places are inside yourself, in the manner of the journals of John Cheever, Sylvia Plath, and May Sarton. Journals lend themselves to brooding, to complaining, to confessions of fear and desire. Diaries are a feminine form, journals seem masculine, but perhaps this is simply because the tangible objects, in my mind, dictate this—diaries with flowery or fabric covers, small locks, pocket-sized; journals seem sturdier, leather-bound perhaps, or like notebooks a scientist might use, like Darwin's cumbersomely named *Journal of Researches into the Natural History and Geology of the Countries Visited During the Voyage of HMS Beagle Round the World, Under the Command of Capt. Fitz Roy, RA.* An excerpt from Darwin's journal reads, "I was, on the whole, disappointed with this ascent [of the Sierra de la Ventana in Argentina]. Even the view was insignificant;—a plain like the sea, but without its beautiful colour and defined outline."

The journal I kept while traveling for two months around Europe in 1984 was transitional, a hybrid of my girlish diary entries and introspective moments similar to my later journals. The pages were filled with

places I traveled and lists of foods I'd eaten, like the conch stew in Oost-
ende, Holland, in which a plug of pale smooth, muscular meat—the
conch—floated in a nearly clear broth, and when I brought the spoon to
my mouth, a clear, sticky strand not unlike the slime trail of a slug dangled disgustingly. I remember writing in the journal religiously at night
before I went to bed, like brushing my teeth, sitting on a lumpy mattress
in some youth hostel or cheap sixth-floor walk-up hotel in Paris or Amsterdam. I traveled with my sister, Susan, and my friend, Kathy, for the
first three weeks of the trip, before I went off alone, and I recall they
mocked my earnest dutiful task of recording our trip. So, in return, I
mocked them and myself. "Dear Monique," I would say aloud when I
opened the blank page, a French nom de plume I'd adopted for the journal: *Sue acted like a big jerk today,* I'd pretend to jot. I purposely excluded
them from this conversation with myself, as if they'd be jealous.

My journals followed me to Michigan, where in 1984 I moved with
my boyfriend, Steve. The notes are inconsistent until 1987 when I wrote
nightly in epistolary form. "Dear Steve," I scrawled in pencil in a lined
notebook, "I miss you so much. I can't believe you are gone. I love you."
Night after night, letters to my dead lover, dead at thirty-one from cancer. I reread this journal only once. I cannot imagine reading it ever again.
When I look at the cover, I know what's inside and I don't want to visit
that raw longing again. Unlike my connection to my other journals, I do
not feel any affection for that particular misery.

In 1995, I wrote obediently in a journal when I lived alone in a small
cottage on Cape Cod during the off-season. It was the first time in my
life, at age thirty-five, that I had lived alone. I quit my job as a fundraiser
for an environmental group to follow my dream of writing, which had
truly been a "dream" since childhood, duly noted in my high school year-
book as my "life goal." Why it took me so long to get started is another
story altogether, but my midlife departure from a career I had established
was an attempt to convert the dream, finally, into a reality. The nine
months living alone without a job or a community or family or friends
nearby were a test—could I withstand what I imagined to be the great
solitude of a writer's life? And a second test—could I write? Could I sustain an idea through to a realized work?

The journal was more of a log, so regular was my attending to it. Like
Darwin's observations of finches, my journal was almost scientific, or at

least anthropological; I studied myself like a creature. In the spirit of May Sarton's quietly affecting *Journal of Solitude*, I wanted to record my experience of isolation, observing myself like a laboratory monkey. (Such creatures, when deprived of love and company, turn neurotic and self-destructive, chewing away at their own flesh. I admit that in my aloneness, I engaged in neurotic behaviors—scratching my scalp distractedly while watching television until, to my horror, I drew blood—though far less extreme than the rhesus monkeys). Seven years later, from these daily journal entries, I began to write of that experience. In fashioning an essay called "Miss Somebody," I imported verbatim text from the journal into the body of the piece.

In 2008, more than a decade after that experience, the essay was published in a journal called *Passages North*. Recently, my colleague Anthony assigned his students to read "Miss Somebody," and then invited me to speak with them. They asked me smart questions about writing the essay, such as where the material came from, and how I remembered details. I told them I had recorded that year in a journal, then said something like, "Most of what I wrote in my journal was dross. I selected the best bits for the essay." I told them that Thoreau wrote seven drafts of his journal, *Walden*, and that editing your journal entries is an acceptable practice in creative nonfiction. The students had been required to keep a journal, to use the journal to respond to various prompts, and record their thoughts and observations. I asked them if the journal entries had provided good fodder for their essays. Several students nodded vigorously.

Later, I began to think about persona, creating a character on the page that is you. My journal is one sort of persona *(Le Misérable)*, and when I pick and choose among its entries and import them into an essay or memoir, it's another level of removal from my real self, or perhaps a fragment of my real self. Sometimes I feel that all I am is persona. I personify a teacher (not what I set out to be, but a way to support my writing habit). I personify a writer, like the day I visited my colleague's class. It seems I'm always trying to answer the same lifelong question—who am I?

Phillip Lopate, in his introduction to *The Art of the Personal Essay*, wrote that writers must deliver or discover "as much honesty as possible," and that the writer should strive to "awaken that shiver of recognition—equivalent to the frisson in horror films when the monster looks at himself in the mirror." My journals contain pure raw angst and anger and desire poured onto the page (so hastily and almost desperately that I often cannot read my own handwriting when I look back). They are, in some ways, more truthful than the memoirs and essays I fashion of this material, or even the stories I tell my family and friends. My journals reflect back to me a monster, of sorts, a Mr. Hyde, the worst of myself. Maybe a better analogy is a reverse Frankenstein's monster. The creature was, on the outside, hideous and beastly, but the person within was sensitive, intelligent, and articulate. I'm an inside-out Frankenstein, appearing to be a kind, decent, normal, professional, responsible person. Sane. But in my journals the creature comes out—the egoist, the narcissist, the whiner, the critic, the petty one, the stingy one, and the mean one. (The creature was awakened even in my youthful diary where I wrote "I hate Beth" and "Lisa Higgins is a flirt and an asshole.") I should burn those journals, those notes to myself. But I must be like Shelley, too, the creator of the creator of the monster. We are all these selves, past and future, as Woolf recognized. The self we create on the page is a refraction, an angle, like when someone is taking a photo of me and I tilt my head down slightly to hide a developing pouch under my chin, angle my head just so, and smile without showing yellowing teeth.

If you read my journals, you might think my life a tragedy for all the heartbreak that is recorded on the pages. In *Poetics*, Aristotle recognized the value in tragedy. He borrowed a medical term, *purgation* (purge, cleanse, purify—referring to the shedding of *katamenia*, or menstrual fluid). He applied this term, *catharsis*, to the audience's experience after viewing a tragedy. Spectators feel "terror" and "pity" while they watch tragic events unfold, which Aristotle thought both pleasurable and therapeutic. "It is the human soul that is purged of its excessive passions," he wrote. Once the feelings are released cathartically, it seems, a sort of balance, or even peace, is restored.

The term has evolved over the millennium. Catharsis can be achieved through ritual or reenactment (at its worst, with scapegoats); or in Freudian psychology through talking about underling causes of trauma; or even in dreams, where we enact lust or violence without consequence. I think of catharsis as an expelling or ridding of that which is causing misery or despair. My journals, then, my compendiums of misery, are the catch basins. It is on those pages that the song of complaint, the song of myself, is recorded. Pain and sadness are expurgated, bled from my gut.

Once outside of me, once my mind is emptied onto the page, I can then examine what was issued or called forth, and later, often years later, I can make some sense of it. I can use the journal notes as raw material, as in my essay, "Miss Somebody."

Catharsis, or purging, has a spiritual enactment as well, in which the body is purified so that the soul may ascend into a state of ecstasy. Scholars of Aristotle theorized that catharsis was pleasurable because the audience experienced *ekstatis,* the root of ecstasy, which means, "trance." In journaling, raw emotion is extruded into words on the page, which are then lifted and transformed through the imaginative process of creation, then reexperienced, tasted again, but from a distance, in a way that is pleasurable. This transformation—the release, return to, and reshaping of pure-bodied emotions I spill into my journal; this attempt to make meaning; to make art from raw experience—traces the journey from despair to ecstasy. The monster is made human.

SEA OF BLUE INK

Kathryn Wilkens

The young man drove 256 miles away from his hometown, about as far as he could go on a tank of gas. He stopped in a station to buy more, but funneled it into a can instead of the car. A few blocks away, in a school parking lot, he doused the car with the gasoline, doused himself, climbed in the trunk, pulled shut the lid, found his plastic lighter and struck flame.

Tears well up in my eyes as I write those words, but they don't spill onto the page as they did nine years ago when I wrote about my nephew in my journal. Although his wasn't the first death I'd recorded—I'd already lost my father, my mother and two close friends—he was the first person whose birth *and* death I'd written about. I went to my cache of books, found the 1978 volume, and read the entry acknowledging a new baby in the family, James. Several months later I'd written that Jimmy was a peaceful child, always smiling when he woke up from his afternoon nap.

The account of Jimmy's death was the most difficult thing I'd ever written, but doing so forced me to acknowledge this new reality. The grieving process is long, and only the passage of time can sand off the jagged splinters of pain. But, because of my journal, denial wasn't an option. Setting down the horrific facts of his death on paper was the first step in accepting the unacceptable.

My journal's beginning was inauspicious. In September of 1975, I picked up a blue ballpoint pen and wrote in a black-and-white speckled composition book, "The purpose of this journal is to record parts of my life I might otherwise forget." The only audience I had in mind was my future self, who, at some point, would read and savor these fragments of memories. I wrote about ordinary events: my teaching job, car trouble, parties, arguments, camping trips, concerts, conversations, and confrontations. I soon found it to be a valuable tool to help sort out personal problems and weigh the pros and cons of important decisions.

I had no plans to maintain a journal forever. Yet each time I came to the final page of a book, closed it, and locked it in the cedar chest, I would spend a few days feeling unmoored, like a vacant rowboat bobbing on a lake. Those feelings vanished as soon as I bought another hardbound journal, which measures 12 ¼ by 7 ¼ inches and has the word *Record* written on the cover.

Many journalers prefer to write in spiral notebooks, but I like the permanence of a bound book. A notebook would make it too tempting to rip out a page after making an error. It's better to think a bit and not make many mistakes in the first place. And when rereading past journals, I'm sure I would have yanked out entire sections and discarded them. The integrity of a bound book forces me to keep the strikeouts as well as the embarrassing emotions. They are all part of the process. I like the idea that my journal is an entity. As I write, I'm creating a lasting artifact.

To maintain continuity, I title each volume. It was a chance occurrence that made me decide to do this. I'd already filled up three books. My grandmother, who grew up on a tobacco farm in Kentucky, gave me a family Bible that had belonged to her mother. On the flyleaf, next to the birth dates of her children, she'd written, "1923, Locust Year." Struck by the succinct evocativeness of those two words, I immediately went to the cedar chest and retrieved my completed volumes. I leafed through and found phrases that summed up what those years had been about.

I've titled every subsequent book, using a few words from the text. Sometimes I know as soon as a phrase comes from my pen that it will end up being the title. Other times I jot down some possibilities on the last page, and choose the best one later. Looking back over my list of titles enables me to see the course my life has taken. The covers of my journals vary—they are black, red, green, blue, and gray. However, inside the words are all in blue ink; I'm not sure why, but no other color is capable of expressing my thoughts. A friend once told me she wrote entries in turquoise, orange, purple or red, depending on her mood. But I stay true to free-flowing blue.

Over the years, I've tried different writing strategies. One summer I vowed to write every single day, but that made me view writing as a chore rather than a privilege. Now I generally write two or three times a week. In 1985, when I bought my first computer, I decided to switch to a data-file format. That didn't last long. I missed writing while curled up in a big chair or in a hammock in my back yard. After realizing that I also preferred the physical act of handwriting to pecking at a keyboard, I reverted back to pen and book—low-tech maybe, but more user-friendly and portable.

When I'd been writing in my journal long enough to see its value, I began teaching a high school elective course in journal writing. At the beginning of each class I suggested several topics, but students were always free to generate their own. On Fridays we counted the pages we'd written and the students selected one or two pages to copy and hand in. Even after budget cuts killed the elective courses, the teachers in my department used journaling as a component of regular English curriculum. We knew students would learn to write faster—and enjoy it more—if they had the freedom to write whatever they wished in addition to the structured assignments we'd given them.

It was rewarding when former students came back to tell me that they were still keeping a journal. One male student who didn't return is one I will always remember. Robert was a freshman, and the only boy on campus allowed to wear a baseball cap inside the classroom. He was completely bald as a result of chemotherapy. Sadly, his cancer resurfaced, and Robert died a few years later. His mother wrote me a letter to say how much she treasured the journal he had kept while in my class, especially the entries he'd written about his grandparents and other family members.

About a decade ago, around the time of my nephew Jimmy's death, I began to see that the journal was more than a record of life. By then I'd completed seventeen volumes, and when I read recent ones and compared them to earlier ones, I saw irrefutable evidence of change and growth. Gradually, the stilted, noun-heavy, term-paper prose of the first volumes was supplanted by a more informal, flowing style. Somewhere along the line—impossible to pinpoint the exact moment—my adult voice had gradually emerged. My writing now had a less apologetic tone. I had become more self-assured but still wasn't selfless. I'd become a little smarter but was far from wise. My writing was quirky, detailed, down-to-earth, and on occasion, even funny.

I wondered if I could write something suitable for publication. Maybe, if I had enough time to flesh out and polish my ideas. Teaching full time meant I had too many lessons to plan and too many papers to grade. At least those were the excuses I gave myself.

Then, quick as a jab from Oscar de la Hoya, it hit me. Whenever I settled in with my journal and lamented the lack of time to write, *I was writing*. I couldn't deny the preponderance of evidence—books and books that swam in a sea of blue ink. I was already a writer. My journal had turned me into one. Through hours of writing practice, I'd experimented with different forms. I had learned to plunge beneath the surface of events. Recounting exchanges with friends and strangers taught me how to write dialogue. I knew how to use strong verbs, and specific language instead of generalities. I could paint a visual picture of a scene, and use the other senses to recreate setting. I could connect the dots of unrelated incidents into a pattern to show their significance. I could lay out an anecdote in a straightforward, unvarnished way. I knew how to heighten drama without distorting the truth. As each journal entry had a beginning, middle and end, I had learned how to shape a story and bring it full circle.

It was time to begin submitting my work. I pored over *Writer's Market* and summoned my courage. I sent an essay to the *Walking Magazine*. A few weeks later, an editor phoned to say she'd accepted it. I wrote a travel article and the *Los Angeles Times* published it (with a gazillion edits). I e-mailed a memoir to an online magazine and later read my story on the Internet. Of course, many rejections also landed in my mailbox, but only the acceptances matter now.

Then the mining began. I sifted through old journals searching for bits that sparkled in the dark. In the journal where I wrote about my mother's death, I found material to shape into an essay. It was about a French-knotted rug she had begun as a young bride and finished late in life. The rug, so many years in the making, became a metaphor for my gradual acceptance of her death.

In my journals, I found humorous anecdotes about my husband's 1971 Mercury Comet that I strung together into an essay that also appeared in the *Los Angeles Times*. A description of monarch butterflies I'd written while on vacation near Big Sur became a central symbol in a how-to article later published in *Writers' Journal*. When I biked in Natchez Trace National Park and decided to write about the experience, I used journal entries written during two earlier trips to round out the article. I had no intention of publishing anything about a road trip taken in 2004, but I was so impressed with the Hotel Pattee in Perry, Iowa, that I sat in the lobby and jotted my impressions in my journal. When I got home, I had plenty of material for a short article. Other travel pieces were easy to compile once I'd done interviews and gathered facts—it was exactly the kind of writing I'd been doing in my journal for years.

At one point, it occurred to me that my journaling experience might be useful to others. Rather than looking at individual entries for ideas, I searched through my journals for trends and techniques. I'd frequently written about nature. I often sprinkled humor in my pages to temper a mundane or gloomy tone. Whereas my earlier entries often began with lifeless statements such as "Well, today wasn't the best day," in later entries I made a point of starting with a sentence I'd never written before. I developed these ideas into articles advising beginning journalers to write about the natural world, to incorporate humor in their writing, and to start each entry with a salient first sentence. And even if your journal is not meant to be read by others, I advise beginners to make it interesting enough so you don't bore yourself during future readings.

My journal gives me freedom to write without restrictions. I can shun punctuation, scrawl sentence fragments or leapfrog from one topic to another. This free-writing generates ideas for essays. While exploring the guilty pleasure of jigsaw puzzles, I ended up with several rambling pages, which I later condensed into an essay. Likewise, I have published first-person pieces about roses, playing Scrabble, dunes, solving Sudoku, ice skating, painting houses, dictionaries and the old, gnarled fig tree growing in my yard.

Although up until now my published pieces have been essays and articles, in the future I may want to branch out. There's no doubt that my journals will provide grist for stories and poems. And if I decide to write a book-length memoir, I am already halfway there. My journal has helped me stay on track in my writing and personal life. Decisions, plans, and goals that are written down aren't easily ignored or forgotten. The journal also serves as a memory-jogger and fact-checker. I might remember that the Los Angeles riots were in April, but was it 1991 or 1992? I find my account in the 1992 volume. I can rely on my journal when I can't rely on my perfidious memory.

At first I thought no one else would read my journal, but now I see it as part of the family archive. Because I write about world events as well as daily life, my journal is a historical document. I wrote nearly all day on

September 11, 2001, chronicling events as they unfolded, citing details that probably won't appear in history books. Whoever reads my account will learn that the military response to the World Trade Center attacks was initially called Operation Infinite Justice, and that on the evening of September 11 members of Congress amassed on the steps of the Capitol and sang an impromptu, a cappella rendition of "God Bless America."

The question is, which will last longer, my published pieces or my journal? Although copies of the publications that carried my words are extant in libraries, and electronic traces remain in cyberspace, probably most of the newspapers and magazines are quietly disintegrating in landfills. But I can't imagine my heirs discarding a collection of books with titles like *Spindrift, Let There Be Latte,* and *Sky in the Shape of Spain.* Inside those books they will find family milestones duly recorded: births, divorces, weddings, graduations, promotions, celebrations, and funerals. My journals as a family legacy will be more important, ultimately, than the published pieces that have arisen from them.

I feel both estranged from and sympathetic toward the young woman who started keeping a journal in 1975. She was often foolish and unfocused. The things she worried about then seem unimportant now. As she poured her confessions, depressions, and obsessions into the journal, it became the vessel for her emergence as an autonomous human being.

In fact, if my journal made me a better writer, it's not much of a stretch to think it made me a better person. It served as a sounding board for new ideas; putting them on paper gave me a chance to examine and evaluate them. Because I complained in my journal, I didn't have to whine to family and friends. It helped me clarify my values as well as my needs and desires. Through it, I've accepted blame, whenever warranted, for things that haven't gone my way. It helped me shake off the past—it's there on paper so it doesn't have to replay in my head. It taught me not to repeat behaviors that had a negative outcome.

Even now, before I begin writing in a new journal, I fan through the pristine pages, ruled with faint aquamarine lines, and try to imagine what comedies, tragedies, or ordinary events will appear over the course of the next year or two. It gives me satisfaction to know that words will come into existence on those very pages, words that will continue my life's narrative.

I look back on all the completed volumes, written in a sea of blue ink. The moods undulate, now heaped up in a crest of success, excitement, and happiness, now sinking into a trough of frustration, boredom, and hopelessness. The lows and highs drift by in a regular pattern, each hollow trough followed by a foam-covered crest. That's the nature of waves, and of life. I wish my nephew Jimmy had known that despair doesn't last forever. Even more, I wish he had kept a journal. He might have found a place to vent his rage instead of turning it against himself.

A personal journal can be many things. It can be a record of life events, a sounding board, or a tool for personal growth. Our passionate scribbling is both writing practice and raw material for future publications. For me, the journal has been all those things, as well as a source of pride and a lifelong commitment. I have no plans to quit. As long as they manufacture Record books and blue pens, I'll keep on writing.

Part 3

THE JOURNAL FOR TRAVEL

I never travel without my diary. One should always have
something sensational to read in the train.

Oscar Wilde, *The Importance of
Being Earnest,* act 2

FROM AN AUDIENCE OF ONE TO AN AUDIENCE OF ANYONE

Wendy Call

M y journal is like a nest, a tangle of shiny trinkets and bits of string: words, sentence fragments, disconnected paragraphs, pages torn from magazines, photographs, even small objects glued into holes I've carved in the pages. Every writer has her obsessions—one of mine is nest building. I'm fascinated by the ways we create the physical and emotional place called *home*. It is built one stick, one glinting thing, a single thread at a time. Dorothy Allison calls her writer's journal "a witness, a repository, and playground." My journal has a similar range of purpose. It is a wailing wall, a laboratory, and junk drawer.

Like the messy closet that stays firmly shut when company comes over, my journal is a private space. Yet, here's the truth of the matter: if I weren't a private journal keeper, I wouldn't be a public writer. Ideas and images form first on my journal's pages, then migrate into the writing I show to the world. They must travel a great distance: from an audience of one to an audience of anyone. How do those words change as they make the journey? When we write for publication, we "should be as honest and explicit as we are with ourselves," says John Updike, because our "words enter into another's brain in silence and intimacy." Updike's counsel has hung with me, haunted me, even hounded me as I fasten my own words to the page. His suggestion is a bold one: make a transcript of one's thoughts and display it for the world to see. Reading is an intimate act, he asserts, so we should be as explicit in public writing as we are in the private world of the mind.

Though I can see the logic of Updike's assertion, I stumble over the word *honest,* the crux of his statement. What does it mean for writing to be honest? Updike might simply be instructing us to tell the whole and unvarnished truth. But does *be honest* mean *tell the truth?* According to the frayed 1969 *Random House Unabridged* that I keep by my desk, "truthful" is the seventh definition of *honest;* before it there are a half-dozen definitions and synonyms, including sincere, frank, genuine, and unadulterated. That last word resonates: *unadulterated* is the perfect word to describe journal writing. The sentences in my journal are those laid down fresh, unencumbered, and undamaged by the internal and external censors that buzz around our words as we polish them for public display.

Honesty is a subject I return to frequently in my journal. I wonder how I can be more honest, lament my lapses, and rage at the dishonesty of others. When I reread old journal entries, I often find myself casting around for a response to the question conjured by Updike's dictum: *How can writing be as honest as thinking?* Like most journal keepers, I sometimes find that my private scribbles tell a truth too whole to bear much rereading. The words in my journal prick the public bubble of identity I've constructed for myself: a well-adjusted person who is curious about the world and its people. My journal reveals a hypersensitive worrier, a hypochondriac, a whiner who repeats the same banal complaints over and over again. But at least that person says what is on her mind. For better or for worse, she's the unvarnished me.

So unvarnished, in fact, she is sometimes unrecognizable. The goal of free-writing, of course, is to stay ahead of the internal critic who carps: *Who are you to assert such a thing? What will the neighbors think? What will readers think?* For me, the trick works; the words that pour onto my journal's pages seem as separate from me as water from air. I didn't become a regular journal keeper, nor a writer, until I was taught the technique of free-writing. From the time I was eight years old until I turned twenty-eight, my journaling followed more or less the same pattern. I would keep a journal for a few weeks or months, then set it aside. When I returned to it, my words embarrassed me so much that I would bury them deep in the detritus of my closet, or shred them into silent confetti. Then, in a workshop I took on a whim, a teacher introduced me to the concept of automatic writing. I no longer felt that I had to take responsibility for whatever spilled onto the page. My not-quite-conscious mind seemed a person distinct from the self I knew. I must thank those champions of free-writing—Louise Dunlap, Peter Elbow, Natalie Goldberg—for giving me the tool that allowed me to write.

When rereading the jumbled entries in my journal, I deeply appreciate the five or twenty-five drafts between journal and publication. When I write for public consumption, I begin a new piece by pulling a few sentences from my free-writing, weaving them into paragraphs, and then knitting paragraphs into a first draft. When a transition or elaboration stumps me, or I stop to wonder—*What am I trying to say here?*—I return to my journal, finding my way word by free-written word.

As a product of my subconscious, my journal cannot help but truth-tell. In my public writing, I endeavor to be truthful, even as I realize there is no such thing as the whole truth. Each of us can access only a sliver of it. Still, the question haunts me: *How can writing be as honest as thinking?* I turn to the most time-honored book of writing advice I know: Lu Chi's *Wen Fu: The Art of Writing.* Seventeen hundred years ago, Lu Chi, a calligrapher, literary scholar, and writer, spent a decade hidden away on a mountaintop, studying Confucian, Taoist, and Buddhist classics. Later he composed a book of writing advice in verse. *Wen Fu* tells us: "Truth is the tree trunk; / style makes beautiful foliage."

Lu Chi goes on to warn: "Where truth and virtue are threatened, / I must surrender / even my favorite jewels." Or, as contemporary writers like to say, *kill your darlings.* Some lines from my journal become favorite jewels; I insert them into drafts of one essay after another, eventually deleting them, still hoping to someday find a place for them. Finally, I must concede that they already had a permanent home, in the journal where they first sprang from my subconscious. I don't kill my darlings, I merely tuck them away in a dark corner of my sprawling nest.

My words' convoluted journey from private journal to published work makes me intensely curious about the journals of well-known writers. The published journal might seem like a lazy literary form, but it appeals to me as one of the most honest. Two long shelves in my office are devoted to published writers' journals. I hold on to the hope that these journals will tell me something important about their authors. Released into the world with the author's coy wink or sheepish grin, or long after he or she is dead, the published journal shows how we are when home alone, in our own skin, pen in hand. That's what home is, or should be: the place where one's actions can be as honest as one's thoughts.

On the shelf below the once-private thoughts of Adrienne Rich, Hannah Hinchman, Henry David Thoreau, and Henry James, thirty-nine of my travel-weary, bent-spine tomes are lined up in chronological order. My journals represent a decade's worth of thoughts. Although I consider my journals honest, the primary emotion I feel when rereading them is not naked exposure, but bewilderment. I write in my journal to grab thoughts and anchor them in the world of dust motes and molecules. If I don't write thoughts down, they decompose, float away, sublimate—passing like iodine into purple vapor. The ideas shimmer with honesty; they seem frank, unadulterated and truthful. When I go back and read what I've scribbled down fast, I can identify some of the thoughts as my own only because they appear in my journal, in my handwriting. It's a paradox—my most honest thoughts are those I don't even recognize as my own.

If my most honest writing is done with the least conscious thought, perhaps the best definition of *honest*, for the purposes of Updike's edict on writing, is *uncensored*. We are most likely to render our true thoughts when we're working too quickly to consider the ramifications of doing so. Joan Didion says of her journal, "The common denominator of all we see is always, transparently, shamelessly, the implacable 'I.' . . . We are talking about something private, about bits of the mind's string too short to use, an indiscriminate and erratic assemblage. . . ." Like birds, we each create a unique nest, one that wouldn't suit anyone else.

Unlike birds, we can carry our nests around with us. I always have a journal with me, whether I'm going away for a month or going to the corner store. When I'm traveling, I make a quasi home between my journal's covers. Though I'm a person who often loses things, I can remember misplacing my journal only three times in the past decade. Each time, it felt like forgetting my own phone number, or getting off the bus and not knowing which way to turn for home.

Because I'm a traveler, away more often than not, my journal is often my only semblance of home. It becomes, quixotically, a repository for the lies I tell. My journal is my confessional, the only one that knows for sure when I've told the truth and when I've lied. Here is one example, written while I was living in a small town in southern Mexico. I was so different from the people around me, I had to find ways to simplify my identity, which meant telling small lies.

September 16, 2001, 9:46 A.M.

I'm in a world that I tell all kinds of lies to. I am a journalist, I'm married, I'm from California, I'm from Boston, I don't drink, the list could go on and on. Sometimes the lies are pointed out to me later and I realize they have slipped out automatically. Like the one in response to, "What church do you belong to?" I try to come up with something as close to the truth as possible, to minimize the lying. For a while I settled on, "My family is Protestant," but then I thought of people imagining me in the pink church across the street that drones out off-tone music and off-beat sermons as early as 7 A.M. and as late as 1 A.M., and it seemed better to try and figure out a way not to answer at all.

I recorded the oversimplifications, small lapses, and white lies in my journal, so that I could remember. This practice brings me back to John Updike's advice: "When we write for publication, we should be as honest and explicit as we are with ourselves." And then I look to Lu Chi for an answer to my nagging question: Can writing really be completely honest? Or can it only be uncensored? Across eighteen centuries, he gives me an unequivocal *maybe:*

> The truth of the thing
> lies inside us,
> but no power on earth can force it.
> Time after time,
> I search my heart in this struggle.
> Sometimes a door slowly opens;
> sometimes the door
> remains bolted.

My journal is a tiny wedge in that door, keeping a splinter of light between latch and jamb, faintly illuminating the rooms of my mind and the nooks and notches of my nest. Even the beginning of this essay about journal keeping came from my journal—although it took more than eight years to find its way out.

References

Baker, Nicholson. *U and I: A True Story.* New York: Random House, 1991.
Didion, Joan. "On Keeping a Notebook," in *Slouching toward Bethlehem.* New York: Farrar, Straus & Giroux, 1968.

Dunlap, Louise. *Undoing the Silence: Six Tools for Social Change Writing.* Oakland: New Village Press, 2007.

Elbow, Peter. *Writing with Power.* New York: Oxford University Press, 1998.

Goldberg, Natalie. *Writing Down the Bones.* Boston: Shambala, 1996.

Junker, Howard, ed. *The Writer's Notebook.* San Francisco: HarperCollins West, 1995.

Lu Chi. *Wen Fu: The Art of Writing.* Translated by Sam Hamill. Minneapolis: Milkweed Editions, 2000.

WRITING IN
PUBLIC PLACES

Bonnie Morris

There are still bookstores and there are still books, mankind's most important invention; there are still readers who prefer the bound volume to the wretched electronic imitation with its sucking dependence on electricity. There is still a body of American literature. But writing books of lasting value that illustrate people's lives in a particular time and place is partly an inborn talent, partly a skill that takes years of development. The mature writer, however deficient in technological ability, possesses a knowledge of human behavior that is gained only through long observation and the toothmarks of sharp experience. (Annie Proulx, *San Francisco Chronicle Book Review,* November 19, 2000)

I

When the journal-writing habit seizes you and sets you on its path, you will need certain things for the rest of your life, whether you use an oak-paneled study, your mother's kitchen, or a rickety jungle tree house as your writing nook. You will need:

Pens for every coat and knapsack and handbag that you own.
A chauvinistic loyalty to your brand of instrument: Bic, Biro, Cross, Waterman, Scheaffer; felt-tip, roller ball, fountain, fine-point, crayon. And mechanical pencil, too, for the creative engineers among you.
Ink. Choose colors that won't fade; this is your stab at immortality, if you can handle the thought of great-grandchildren or grad students reading your account of certain nude pool parties or that first mammogram/prostate exam.

Real paper, creamy, heavyweight, spiral—later, if you wish, you may certainly transfer journal entries to a cold and blinking screen. But the paper in your lap permits your moving hand to caress both pen and surface, a workmanship format centuries old, irreplaceably intimate. Know your own handwriting. Whose *g* is that? Your father's? Or lifted from that kid you admired in youth group?

A writing place and time, a favorite nook or bench, a willingness to create writing space in chaos, solitude in crowds—the ability to write in jail, on subways, during revolutions, at rock concerts, in bed.

If you like, a tape recorder and a camera rounding out the sounds and sights, interviews and images that collectively inspire you to capture or describe your life.

Most important of all—you will need the ability to survive, as a writer, through the unforeseen and difficult times without any of the luxuries just described.

II

A secret tribe of journal keepers exists out there, people seemingly placed on this earth to describe, record, and savor, pen in hand. Yes, I am one of these watchful, scribbling folk. At forty-six, I've filled one hundred and forty-six 300-page journals since age twelve, and am finally ready for the conversation I long to spark with other writers. Why do we do it? How do other people ever put up with us? How many relationships have floundered because we really prefer uninterrupted writing time and the company of a spiral notebook? What nerds we journal-keepers are!

When you genuinely love and look forward to writing, it's not enough to breathe, to believe, to breed, to earn a fine living, to round out your human lifespan with sports and food and movies; you have to write stuff down. You feel charged with strange obligations—to remember, and to create memory, to observe, but also to participate, writing yourself into the story, perhaps.

A quiet life may suddenly grow epic. Some journal entries declare, "I had no idea I'd be writing today's diary in a lifeboat," or "Well! We seem to have been stopped by the border police, so I think I'll use the time to describe last night's orgy."

If you are female, whether a little girl or an outrageous grownup, your need to write will strike some as defiance; women are evaluated and rewarded for expressing with their bodies, not with their minds. Female literacy and scholarship remain in too many cultures as forbidden, oxy-moronic. George Orwell's everyman Winston Smith, daring to start his journal in *1984* while knowing such an act of personal agency was for-bidden, was fictitious; not so the Taliban militia of Afghanistan, which closed all schools for girls in the mid-1990s and called female education "immodesty." What is the revolutionary meaning of a girl's journal in Kabul? One might imagine a slender notebook held tightly behind the veil of a hungry child, house windows blacked out by law so no men but the morals police may monitor women's lives.

Too easy, though, to blame totalitarian regimes for squelching creative output. We do it to ourselves here in America; our own pals play their hand at discouraging the writing life. At fourteen, as a middle-class, white girl living in an affluent country, I listened numbly as a circle of other white girls told me I had a choice—give up my journal and be accepted into their gang or keep my private notebook and have neither friends nor protection in our hostile junior high. For two weeks, I stopped writing—the only two weeks I've gone without my journal since 1974. But I'm get-ting ahead of the story.

I write in my journal by hand, with a Sheaffer fountain pen. That organic feel of nib on paper, ink seeping into calloused fingers, college-ruled notebook flopped open on warm knees—that raw immediacy of unedited creation has been replaced, for most of my current students and academic pals, with laptops and Microsoft screens. The last decade of our beloved twentieth century saw a complete restructuring (in developed countries) of what it means to write—onscreen editing, online publish-ing, independent and progressive bookstores and presses driven out by giant conglomerates, freaked-out freshmen explaining that a brilliant paper has been *lost,* swallowed whole, cannot be retrieved, because a disk has "crashed." E-mail is convenient, urging the most misanthropic recluses toward the dailiness of an easy correspondence without stamps; gone are the tenderly handwritten letters sending promises to lovers, par-ents, and friends. Gone is the ten-year-old kid lying on her belly on a shag rug, writing stories; she's upright at her workstation, surfing the informa-tion highway, preparing for college admission, while her toddler brother works a baby keyboard rather than a sixty-four-color Crayola box. A lap-top, though increasingly lightweight, isn't a *real* notebook yet; it can't be crammed into the back pocket of old Levis when one crawls under the beach pier to make out at midnight in July. The spontaneity of journal writing—"Wait, wait, I just need to write this down,"—and the ability to stick an autumn leaf or a movie stub between marked pages has been transformed by technology. For better or worse, this is our wry predicament in space age 2009, an era wherein Sony Computers airs commercials calling a new screen system . . . "the modern version of putting pen to paper."

Like so many writers of my generation—I was born in mid-1961—I was almost finished with graduate school before computers replaced typewriters in the halls of academe. When I began writing my Ph.D. dissertation in winter 1989, I sold my italic typewriter and logged on to user-friendly WordPerfect 4.1. How thrilling it all was: errors disappeared at a button's touch, whole paragraphs shifting tidily like Balanchine's ballerinas, entire manuscripts printing and self-paginating while one was *elsewhere*—at the store, in the bathtub. WordPerfect's flag-blue screen—wholly blank except for the meek reminder of file name and page number—resembled unmarked paper—empty until filled.

Okay, I thought. *I can do this. Okay.*

Within a few years, that crossover ended. The ante went up. WordPerfect's fjordlike blankness was phased out at every institution where I taught, no longer supported in the tech-speak of campus. Everyone was forced to work with Microsoft: screens jammed with colored borders, prompts, icons, menus, each blinking their suggestions—an invading army of options relentlessly presented to the writer. Spell check interrupted my essays and class lessons by highlighting words *it* found all wrong—Latina, Kurdish, kibbutznik, the Michigan Womyn's Music Festival, riot grrl, not to mention my lowercase heroines k.d. lang and bell hooks. I watched as the world of "real" writing grew, like Jack's beanstalk, into something always vertical, the screen station, the electronic path to tenure upright in one's face. Yet, I have remained attached in the deepest way to the horizontal writing life, blank pages in my lap.

These days my students, fresh from an adolescence spent with mouse in hand, find written tests archaic. Why not assign only take-home essays they can edit on the computer? Why should I suffer needlessly through their handwriting in a blue book? They examine my fountain pen with interest, then ask why I don't put my journal entries on disks. Cleverly, they point out that I'll help my future biographers if I organize my memoirs in file form. This spectra of posthumous editing by some worshipful Ph.D. candidate is a morbid thought indeed. Now even immortality requires Windows.

Did we ever expect to arrive at this crossroad, the end to a millennium of handwriting? Even the Bible speaks of the scribe's joy—"My heart overfloweth with a goodly matter; my tongue is the pen of a ready writer." Literacy and the religious life were once inseparable—monks, nuns, and rabbis examined their souls endlessly in diaries of spiritual progress and temptation. Travelers, adventurers, explorers, and kings—mostly male, but let's not forget Anne Frank and Gluckel of Hameln—plotted the world (and their own cultural survival) through journals. Has the tattered handwritten journal truly ended, as of our century? Will texts of American history henceforth show that handwriting and typewriters were phased out by 2001? The twenty-first century sits crowded with technology's furniture, quadrupling the time we sit attentive to an electronic presentation. Perhaps my alarm is merely that of the sixties child ever warned by hippie parents not to sit too close to the radioactive television set.

I race to play catch-up as new students arrive each fall, always more computer-literate than the last year's bunch. The disparity in our affection for technology is just a new spin on the old generation gap. Most professors these days agree, however, that our students' nicely printed-out pages and Internet research do not compensate for their increasingly abysmal writing skills—grammar, punctuation, spelling, and the latter-day evils of website plagiarism and online paper-buying. The escalation in affordable technology (though a laptop is still a large financial investment and theft risk) hasn't been accompanied by an escalation in student literacy. The urge to write well for writing's sake seems missing in a generation raised to expect an A for a C⁻ paper.

So these are my biases, revealed up front. I am concerned about the writing sensibility in our time, and my journal is a notebook of the old kind that travels easily with me everywhere I go. I have carried a journal through thirty-eight countries with no fear of its theft, no need of fresh battery packs, though I often dream of losing it at sea. I plug it directly into my mind, sketching or writing or Scotch-taping into it the great minutiae of cultures. The only threats are elemental—fire and water, or leaving it behind. Notebook writing, I have found, invites friendly conversation in ways a laptop says—"Go Away." For instance, I was scribbling away outside the Cairo Museum when a busload of Egyptian schoolgirls arrived and descended on me, each begging to show off her English by signing her name in my notebook. And I once passed an evening sipping tea in a Jerusalem café, painstakingly learning the Armenian alphabet from a witty chef, new word shapes stained with hummus in my journal. It is this crosscultural human contact, made possible through the universal handprint of art and naming, which I hope we will not lose, as nation after nation eagerly follows the Western model of computerized writing. A pen and journal still cost less than admission to a movie. Like Anne Frank, like Hildegard of Bingen, like Martin Luther King, Jr., awake all night in jail, we must be prepared to write our greatest testimony in nontechnical conditions, where and when we can.

III

Journal writing is like sex; do it in a public place and people can't help but stare, even as their attention suggests *you* are behaving in a socially inappropriate way. I've always done much of my writing in public places—parks, coffeehouses, the National Zoo, even curbside at Gay Pride rallies—and the reactions range from accusations of FBI infiltration to genuine concerns that I'm a homeless schizophrenic. Many writers do their best work in public space. I think of screenwriter David Mamet's book *Writing in Restaurants*. Who's the voyeur—the writer taking notes or the passerby gawking at the writer? We don't all have cozy offices at home where we can churn out our latest bestseller while listening to Bach, Barbra, or Basie. But who writes a book while waiting in a bathroom line at the movie theatre? Well, I do, of course.

When I began living in D.C. again and teaching at George Washington University, I didn't have a desk, a view, or a computer of my own. For ten years I lived in a box-sized studio apartment at DuPont Circle with its one long window facing a brick wall. The first two computers I dragged home both died horribly in mid-sentence. Like many nontenured women's studies professors, I shared office space with other valiant faculty; nonetheless, I managed to churn out six books in six years. The secret to my work ethic is no secret at all. I write in my journal, wherever I wish, all the time, and type up the good stuff later.

A date with my journal is the most pleasant of outings. Off we go to the movies, where so many strange childhood memories float to the surface in the twenty minutes before the lights go down. Everyone wonders if I'm a film critic. But no—I'm using that comfy, faux-velvet chair time, Junior Mints melting on my tongue, to write about last week's insult or this year's romance or any number of thoughts. The National Zoo is even better—certainly the animals are nice, but for people watching, the Zoo is just spectacular. What a complex laboratory of dialogue, etiquette, parent-child relations, and tourist culture! "Do you want to go home right now, Stevie?" some fed-up mother is always threatening and spanking. "Why is that monkey touching his popo, Daddy?" another kid shrieks. I bring my Mocha Blast from Baskin-Robbins and settle in for an afternoon of listening and describing—journal time that is both work and play.

It's harder to seize one's writing time in crowds. A veteran of countless women's music festivals, I've come to use my favorite performers' concerts as background music for the journal time I need—the ultimate writing nook being, for me, not a wood-paneled study at all, but a deranged, campfire party hosted by stage techies and sign-language interpreters. It does seem antisocial to write in that setting—but what if you dig being in it and describing it simultaneously? Nothing can surpass the conversations overheard backstage at the Michigan Womyn's Music Festival.

"Are you writing about me?" snarls a stagehand as, desperately blotting ink by firelight, I attempt to describe the day's highlights, plus plan the two-hour women's history workshop I'm to give the next day. "Say, this isn't going in one of your books, is it?"

I once tried to assemble my personal list of the coolest writing places in the world, based on previous eco-challenge-type spots where I'd managed to steal journal time. Halfway up a Pyramid. The Wailing Wall—women's side, of course. Near a hawk's nest right below the "Hollywood" sign. In a jail cell after committing civil disobedience, hands still cuffed behind my back. On the beach boardwalk in Santa Cruz, California. At a remote Berber market run by tattooed women in Morocco. Backstage at an Indigo Girls concert with one of their guitar picks serving as a bookmark. Inside a dead volcano in New Zealand. In these places, I'm the one with the fountain pen dripping, "Oh, my GOD, guess where I am NOW," my writing life charged, inspired, informed by the magic setting. But writing is work, not rejuvenation, to Orthodox Jews; in Israel or Brooklyn, on the Sabbath one may not write. I learned this on my first trip to Jerusalem at age twenty, when I was told to put my pen down by an angry Hasidic rabbi.

Laptops have made accepted public writers of us all. The scruffiest beatnik agitator *looks* upwardly mobile and productive, because we associate computer keyboards with work, in a way we never privileged wild-haired poets scrawling free verse on bar napkins. Because laptops are costly, class bias demands that we judge their owners to be safe. No one disturbs the laptop guy at Starbucks. But is he really *writing*? Creating? Is that his travel diary, his novel? Or is he just filing spreadsheets for his boss? Those who dare intrude might say, "What are you working on?"—not, "What are you *writing*?"

I want laptop man—or woman—to be a real writer, not a drudge. I want all of us to uphold our right to be dreamy in public with glazed-eyed journals in our laps and a grand view of the world. There is no greater partner than one's journal—in tough times and in discrete life stages, it serves as playmate, lover, tour guide, political witness, employer, and spiritual sanctuary, as well as editor and therapist. These are the writing relationships and practices I now look to explore. This is the conversation I now intend to have.

NOTES FROM
AN ACCIDENTAL
JOURNAL KEEPER

Michael Steinberg

In a foreign country the pattern of days is less predictable, each one has its character and is easier to remember. So, too, the weather; and, so, too, the shape and feel of newspapers, the sound of bells, and taste of beer and bread. It is all rather like waking up and not knowing who or where one is . . . quite ordinary things take on an edge; one keeps discovering oneself miraculously alive. (Alastair Reid, *Whereabouts: Notes on Being a Foreigner*)

In June 2007, just before I was about to leave the country to teach a workshop in Prague, the editor of this anthology asked if I'd submit an essay. My first response was to politely decline. The book is, after all, a collection of essays by writers on / about the role of journaling in their creative process, and that description doesn't fit the way I work.

As a rule, I'm not the kind of writer who records his thoughts or expresses his feelings in a journal. Only infrequently do I use a notebook to explore ideas for future writings. Usually, when a thought comes to me, I scribble notes on random scraps of paper or Post-its. When I really have my act together, I jot ideas in a spiral-bound note pad that fits in my shirt pocket. Not the most efficient way, I admit, to organize my thinking.

It's not that I'm journal-allergic. When I took inventory of my past writings, I recalled two instances when I felt *compelled* to keep a journal. The first was in September 1985, when my wife Carole and I made our initial trip abroad to Paris and London. The second time was in 1992 when I taught a class in London.

This gap in my journal-keeping practices made me wonder why seven years had lapsed between my first and second travel journals, even though I had traveled abroad during the time between. When I decided to accept the editor's invitation, I started thinking about those two travel journals. I rummaged around and found them in my old files. Since both were prompted by travel and teaching abroad—and since I'd be teaching in Prague during the summer of 2007—I decided to keep a third journal while there, thinking it might help me examine just what role, if any, my previous journals played, either in my creative process, or in some other capacity, yet unknown to me.

As a memoirist, I've found that once memory and imagination start tracking a thought, an idea, or a feeling, unexpected discoveries begin to emerge. As soon as I'd set myself the challenge of taking on this project, I realized that there was another added benefit to be gotten from it.

For example, in the early spring, I'd begun making notes for a chapter that would become part of a proposed memoir about later, midlife changes. At that time, I had a vague notion that my midlife travels were a catalyst for my uneven transition from being an uncertain and unfocused English professor to someone who today has (hopefully) a more grounded sense of himself as a teacher and writer.

Although I am unsure how those journal entries will be incorporated into my forthcoming memoir, I know that at some point in the future I will refer back to them. In the meantime, after returning home from Prague, I decided to reread all three of my journals in the exact order in which they were composed.

Here are some excerpts from my first travel journal in 1985:

September 3, En Route to Paris

To my utter surprise, I'm enthusiastically reading the guide books, planning our itinerary—the museums and historical sites we'd visit. What restaurants we'd go to. What day trips we'd take. The choices are overwhelming. It's bringing back memories of the anticipation and excitement I used to feel when in college, voraciously reading history and literature, and daydreaming of visiting all the places I was reading about. What ever happened to that adventurous kid, anyway? Where is he now?

September 5, Paris

Being a first-time tourist is exhilarating and humbling. It's all so seductive. How can you avoid trying to do too much—an impulse which has always been a big part of my make-up. Everything is so new and unfamiliar. I tend to idealize it all.

September 6, Paris

This is an adventure and a sensual delight. But also grueling and disconcerting. A new culture, unfamiliar languages and customs. A million mistakes and faux pas. Today, I double-tipped a waiter in a café. I didn't bother to ask if the service was included. And he didn't bother to let me know that it was. When I figured it out, naturally I felt like an ignorant tourist. Maybe I'm not the worldly, perceptive New Yorker I pretend to be.

September 7, Paris

Over indulgence is my middle name—gotta' have this and that—post cards, souvenirs, mementos. I'm the stereotypical American—the modern Pilgrim and his relics. To my dismay, I'm finding out that I fit the description of the typical American consumer—the kind of person I always used to ridicule and criticize. Ouch!

Later on That Day

Walking all over Paris, taking trains, buses, guided tours—L'Orangerie to see the Monet Water Lilies; the Impressionists at Jeu de Paume, and the masterworks at the Picasso Museum—all in one day. On a previous day, the Eiffel Tower, Les Halles, and the Pompidou Center. And in between, day trips to Chartres and Versailles—a whirlwind of activity. Exhilarating, but also draining.

September 8, Paris

No time to relax. This is becoming a kind of crash course—cramming everything into a week. Has its own urgency, its own rhythms independent of ours—of mine, anyway. Carole wants us to slow down. Pick one or two things and really absorb them. Me, I'm in my "What Makes Sammy Run" mode. I want to pack in everything I can. There's a rush of excitement and anticipation that builds up before every new adventure. I feel a pounding in my chest, even as I map out the day's plans.

But, just like overeating or too much sex—you lose the capacity to savor the experience, to reflect on it. Typical New Yorker that I am, I'm not yet attuned to that point of view. My nature is to try and do way too much—always has been. Over here, I've become even more addicted to the adrenaline rush than I was in New York. Carole is right. I need to learn how to take in and focus on one thing at a time.

September 10, Paris

Almost the end of the Paris leg. I notice that I'm beginning to separate the tourists like myself from the natives. I'm comparing my own frantic, scattered rhythm to the more civilized and measured pace they maintain. I watch people of all ages spending part of the day in the beautiful parks and gardens. I observe them talking and having coffee at outdoor cafés. I'm intrigued by the notion that the shops and stores in Paris close for two hours at lunchtime. And that everyone in France gets two six-week vacations—in August and at the beginning of the New Year.

September 11, Last Day in Paris

Am I finally getting the hang of this? Today, we strolled and window shopped on the Rue di Rivoli, went to Bertillon on the Isle de St. Louis for an early afternoon glace [ice cream]. Later on we had an espresso and a pastry at a neighborhood bakery, then a late afternoon picnic— ham, cheese, bread and wine—in Luxembourg Gardens. We sat and read and people-watched. I wish we could have done more of these kinds of things earlier on. At first, slowing down was a respite from all the sightseeing. But now, when it's almost too late, I'm beginning to look forward to these quiet diversions simply for the pleasures they yield on their own. Is this the beginning of a new phase, I wonder?

September 12, First Day in London

When you're on holiday in a foreign country, eating well, day trips to churches, museums, and small villages make it so easy to lose your equilibrium and judgment. Everything seems so new, so romantic. It's a journey into the unknown. You turn a corner and discover something charming or dazzling or overwhelming—like stopping for high tea at the Ritz, or the majesty of the Abbey, or even an elegant meal in a restaurant you happened to stumble upon. It feels so fresh, so exhilarating that you can't help but give yourself over to the fantasy.

It's like you're experiencing these pleasures for the first time. You lose your sense of balance. You feel intoxicated, as if you're living in an unreal dream. What a contrast from the routine, worries, and responsibilities of everyday life. Hold on pal, you're starting to sound like a tourist again, just like you were in Paris.

September 13, London

In London only one day and I'm repeating the same patterns I established in Paris buying postcards, picture books, guide books of all kinds. Taking hundreds of photos. The freedom and adventure is becoming a daily fix. The old me, the me that wants to sample everything is taking over again. I get up early and scribble out the itinerary. Gotta' see the Tower, St. Paul's, the museums, West End plays. And what about the art, and architecture—and the day trips—Hampton Court, Windsor Castle, Oxford. But in my more sober moments—usually at night when I'm dead tired, it's becoming clear that all I can manage is a quick hit and then it's on to the next thing. Sure, I want to learn everything, see everything, and absorb all of it. But sometimes it feels like a frantic desperation. And it's beginning to trouble me.

September 14, London

On the way to Hampton Court and Windsor Palace, we drove through the countryside and saw some of the little villages where the quality of life seems so simple, so peaceful. A respite from the city's pace—the restless energy, compulsion to move from new adventure to new adventure. But today, I'm feeling the way I did on our last afternoon in Paris. I notice that each house, no matter how small or run down, has a tiny garden. Reminds me of the tranquil feelings I get whenever we're in northern Michigan. It's funny, when you're in unfamiliar surroundings, you can appreciate places you've never really thought much about.

It's obvious that I'm over-romanticizing, over-idealizing things again. But I know I need to spend more time with myself. By myself. I need to make my peace with the demons that drive and distract me. Just keeping these journal notes makes me want to write and read more, and work in the garden like Carole. Why has it taken me so long to figure this out? Slow learner, Carole says, just like your father always said.

On the plane ride home, I wrote the following:

I'm ready, I think, to take a closer look at myself. Instead of compulsively buying three newspapers a day to keep up with what's going on, instead, on this trip I read books about Paris and about the history of London. And this journal is proof that I'm beginning to write more frequently, and for longer periods of time. But halfway through the trip, I started to slow myself down—started to take stock. And now, in my mid-forties, I feel ready for a change.

My habit as a writer is to go back through my drafts trying to locate the thoughts, ideas, and feelings that seem to repeat themselves several times over. And that's precisely what I did after rereading my first travel journal. While reading that journal, I could see that my early entries in both Paris and London were predictably about the initial exhilaration of travel—the newness, the unplanned surprises and discoveries; the sensation of feeling both like an uninformed novice and a displaced American. I could feel the palpable presence of centuries of history—the past—the overwhelming influence of religion, art, and architecture; and of course, a renewed realization of my own mortality—pretty much standard fare for the neophyte traveler, I'd say.

I used a yellow magic marker to underline frequent repetitions. The pattern I observed was pretty schizo. It went something like this: an initial exhilaration accompanied by a compulsion to see and do everything juxtaposed with a gradual realization that I needed to slow down and focus—savor the experience.

In retrospect, I believe this was the beginning of a passage (no pun intended)—from a prolonged self-absorption and a compulsive need to be on the move to a more reflective way of looking at things. In fact, after I came back from that first trip, I noticed that I'd written almost a hundred pages of notes in my travel journal.

Toward the end of both segments—Paris and London—I noticed a persistent, recurring idea that had begun to surface: my gradual awareness of the difference between being a tourist, a rookie traveler, and what it might feel like to be a resident—albeit a temporary one—in a foreign city. Over time, as the next two journals will attest, this would become a reality.

In January of 1992 at age fifty-one, I had the first of two cornea transplants. The operations provided me with almost a year's release time from teaching. In retrospect, that enforced sabbatical offered me permission to step away from teaching obligations and normal everyday responsibilities. And for the first time, I was able to focus on my writing.

In the summer of 1992, I was offered the chance to teach in London for six weeks. Curiously enough, that's when I decided to keep my second travel journal. Here are some excerpts from that one:

July 4, 1992, London

Taking my class on the city tour today, I could feel the familiar impulsiveness resurfacing; the need to do and see everything I can before I go back home. The old urgencies still return when I'm in an international city. Living in London reminds me of what it felt like to live in New York. I like it and I don't. Sometimes, I feel like I'm two people. I'm still enamored by all the possibilities here—the plays, the museums, the day trips—the whole nine yards. But this time, something feels different. I'm finding that I miss the reflection and calm that comes when I spend down time at home writing and reading.

July 11, London

After a week here, I'm still pretty disconnected. I like it when I'm out in the city, finding good restaurants, seeing plays on the West End, going to the Tate—and all the other discoveries and surprises a city like this has to offer. But in the last few days, I didn't feel those persistent cravings; the "I want, I want" voice in my head is less insistent.

This is a privileged existence, to be sure. But it doesn't transport me in the same way it used to; it doesn't fully engage me in the same way as it once did. Maybe it's because I've traveled abroad so many times. The city has become less of an addiction and more of a reward for having taught all week.

To my surprise, I even find myself marking time until I can get back to my northern Michigan retreat and my writing. This is the first time since I've been abroad that I've felt that impulse. What I seem to enjoy most these past few years is spending time up north writing and relaxing—walking on the beach and in the woods with Carole; reading and listening to jazz at night; and simply allowing myself time to think and reflect. The eye surgery, it seems, has granted me a kind a second sight—a chance, an excuse, maybe, to slow down and focus on the things I still want to accomplish in the limited time I have left.

July 31, London

For the first time since I've been abroad, I've got a daily routine to anchor me. Living and working here demands a more measured pace in comparison to what it feels like to be here on holiday. Getting up for work each day, taking the underground to the university, stopping for breakfast, shopping for dinner on the way home from class, staying in at night prepping and reading my student's work. I feel more in sync with the fabric of daily life. This is, I know, a different kind of romantic illusion, and so, it marks an interesting shift in priorities from the things that drove me in those early years of travel. I hadn't written any travel journals since 1990.

Here then is an excerpt from two entries from my 2007 visit to Prague:

July 18, Prague

For the five weeks we've lived here, my teaching, daily preparation, the evening readings and talks have dominated my time. We live at the foot of the St. Charles bridge, and except for excursions up the hill to the magnificent Castle that oversees the entire city, and visits to the Kafka museum up the street and to some local churches and historical landmarks, we didn't feel compelled to travel on the weekends—save for a single day trip to the Nazi prison camp/fortress at Terazin—the only place we simply had to see. But now that my teaching gig is over, this morning we talked about the things we still wanted to explore in the few days we had left. And in that moment, the old "let's-see-everything-on-the-list knee-jerk" resurfaced. I found myself compulsively rattling off a litany of things I wanted to see and do before we left—go to the Mozart Museum; see the season ending Mozart concert in the park; attend the final Proms' concert at the Municipal House; and maybe even catch the Rolling Stones concert a hundred miles outside of Prague.

Right in the middle of a sentence, I started to laugh. When I turned to look at Carole, we both knew we weren't going to do any of those things, except perhaps the Proms' concert. And, if we were up to it, maybe an after-concert coffee and pastry in the art deco Kaverenske Café.

In the same breath, we agreed that there's a lot more to learn about this city and its culture. But whatever we didn't see, whatever we didn't get around to doing, we would save for another time. And if there is no other time, then so be it.

July 19, Prague

On our last day, we got up early, and as usual walked to the corner patisserie for an espresso and a croissant (an homage to Paris, maybe?). Then we sat in the park and read the International Herald Tribune, watched the tour boats on the river, took catnaps, and went for a late dinner in a French café we'd been meaning to try since we arrived here three weeks ago.

So what have I learned about the role journals play in my writing routine and in my creative process? As a memoirist, my charge is to examine the past in hopes of coming to a fuller understanding of which experiences, people, encounters, and relationships might have helped shape my choices and decisions.

Here then, are a few final thoughts and observations:

Because my three journals were written over a period that spans some twenty-two years, I can see an ongoing struggle between two opposing sides of my nature—seems to repeat itself over and over again throughout each journal. And if there's a dominant pattern in my behavior and in my autobiographical writings, it would be the struggle to become a more responsible and accountable self.

In this regard, I can see the differences between the me who at forty-five was a rookie tourist, and the more experienced me who just returned after living and teaching in Prague. And despite the fact that all three journals were written at separate intervals and for very different purposes, it's clear that the experience of traveling and living abroad was a catalyst for important midlife changes. The first two journals, in particular, might even qualify as a turning point in my quest to become a more fully formed adult.

I won't claim that I'm a citizen of the world or that I've transformed myself from an impressionable, overly quixotic tourist, to a wise and practical elder statesman. Depending upon the situation and my state of mind, I'm a little bit of both and still evolving.

Having gained a deeper sense of the role these travel journals have played in my writing, I can, however, say with some conviction that the Prague journal won't be the last one I write.

Part 4

THE JOURNAL AS MUSE

What is The Subconscious to every other man, in its creative aspect becomes, for writers, The Muse.

Ray Bradbury, *Zen and the Art of Writing* (1990)

HOLDALLS

John DuFresne

Beside the Seine. These are the loveliest of moments in the notebook, for they expand. The very words I set down here are like the roots underground in winter. They look a little skimpy on the page, but they carry secret pages in them. (James Wright)

You ought to keep a notebook for several reasons. (And you ought to carry it with you.) A notebook is a reminder that you're a writer and that what you're currently doing while you're out of the house, away from the desk, is taking notes toward your next novel. You know that you think differently when you have a pen in your hand—and you observe differently. You see what's really there, not what's supposed to be there. You keep a notebook to teach yourself to pay attention. You keep a notebook to encourage yourself to create. You keep a notebook to serve notice to the world—Writer at Work! When you're writing a novel, it becomes a magnet for everything that happens in your life, and the notebook is where you store what the novel has attracted.

Writing regularly in your notebook keeps the creative juices churning; it preserves thoughts, images, overheard lines, dreams, whatever it is that catches your imagination. A notebook affords you the opportunity to write when you may only have five minutes to do so.

Writing engenders more writing. The image you capture now might show up in the novel you write in ten years. The notebook is the repository and source of writing material; the notebook is a refuge. Open it up when you need to think. Read what you've written; write about what you've just read.

Note-taking can be a creative act. It may not be your purpose to write a novel based on the image you've captured—birds nesting in a human skull—but once you get started, you may just keep writing. You don't need much kindling to fire a novel.

My notebook is an anthology, so to speak. It's not a diary or a journal. You can call it a journal if you must, or a daybook, a commonplace book, a scrapbook. Virginia Woolf called hers a holdall. It is not a daily record of occurrences. A writer's diary might have the same entry every day: "Sat down to write at 9 A.M. Stopped at 8 P.M., had a drink, read, and went to sleep." We don't lead eventful lives except for those lives in our heads. The notebook is not meant to be an obsession, but a tool. Journal writers are not interested in facts, per se, but in stimulation. The notebook is not so much about what happened, as about what could happen.

It's for your eyes only, not for publication. It doesn't need to be neat, orderly, or logical. In fact, it ought to be a mess. You don't need to have a system; only collect! Write down remarks that you hear or what you've read on the craft of writing, conversations overheard in restaurants; collect and tape in newspaper articles or photographs that you might use in a story sometime; write down phrases or words that might become titles or chapter headings or dialogue; list story ideas, titles, names, words, or images. Keep your senses alert and gather your data in the notebook.

The constant use of the notebook keeps you working and writing, and provides a mine of material to be used down the road. Keep anything pertinent to your development as a writer: character sketches, found poems, observations, all of the preliminary stuff for the first stages of the writing process. What you write down now goes toward all the writing you will ever do.

The sentence you overheard—"It's good to be back, but where am I?"—might not be appropriate for the novel you're working on, but might be the seed of the novel you're going to write next. And you don't need to know how that'll come about. Trust in the material. A notebook is a warehouse, not a museum. You're taking it down so it's there when you need it. And you don't need a system—write it all as fast as you can. The notebook is not an end, but a means.

Before we go on, I want you now to get a notebook if you don't have one. We're going to write. I use those blank, lined journals they sell at the chain bookstores. $5.99. Each one is 190 pages or so, and they last for months. I used to use the little three-by-five memo pads—and still do when it's inconvenient to haul the big notebook around. And then at night I would transfer the memo notes to the larger book. A ringed binder will do, loose paper in manila folders will do. (I abandoned that method, however, when the desk got so cluttered I couldn't work. The cat didn't even have room to curl up and sleep.) Use what works for you, but don't go spending a lot of money on a fancy notebook. (Don't judge a notebook by its cover.) It's not supposed to look good. After a while it won't look good. It needs to be durable and functional, not decorative. It's going to get beat up a bit, and you don't want it falling apart. I'll wait here while you go buy or fetch a notebook. Go ahead. We'll take up the next paragraph when you get back.

Chekhov kept a notebook. He titled one of his notebooks "Themes, Thoughts, Notes, and Fragments." Here's an entry:

> At twenty she loved Z., at twenty-four she married N. not because she loved him, but because she thought him a good, wise, ideal man. The couple lived happily; everyone envies them, and indeed their life passes smoothly and placidly; she is satisfied, and, when people discuss love, she says that for family life not love nor passion is wanted but affection. But once the music played suddenly, and, inside her heart, everything broke up like ice in spring; she remembered Z. and her love for him, and she thought with despair that her life was ruined, spoilt for ever, and that she was unhappy. Then it happened to her with the New Year greetings; when people wished her "New Happiness," she indeed longed for new happiness.

Here's why you needed to find a notebook. Right now you get to write this story in your notebook, the one that Chekhov never got around to writing.

Only your story happens this year in your town. (When Chekhov used an entry from his notebook, he crossed it out. And he would recopy entries from one book into another—this was a serious matter for Chekhov.) More correctly, you get to begin to take notes about the story. And when you're finished, here are some more provocations from the master, all from his notebooks:

> A pregnant woman with short arms and a long neck, like a kangaroo.
>
> A serious phlegmatic doctor fell in love with a girl who danced very well, and, to please her, he started to learn a mazurka.
>
> He flatters the authorities like a priest.

The ice cream is made of milk in which, as it were, the patients bathed.

One of the most fascinating notebooks is not a writer's, but artist Leonardo da Vinci's. His notebooks were "mirror written," backwards from right to left. In his notebooks were notes on anatomy, music, painting, and sculpture; remarks about light; ideas for future projects; reminders about neighbors in possession of certain rare books; drawings; natural observations, such as "The shadows of plants are never black, for where the atmosphere penetrates there can never be utter darkness"; exercises, such as "Describe the tongue of the woodpecker and the jaw of the crocodile"; and sententiae, like this:

> He who walks straight rarely falls.
> We are deceived by promises and time disappoints us.
> He who thinks little, errs much.
> The greatest deception men suffer is from their own opinion.

As I said, I use those 8 ½-by-11, hardbound notebooks. The first thing I do in the morning is pour my coffee and read through the newspaper looking for material (and checking the Red Sox score). When I find a story, I cut it out and use a glue stick to paste it into the notebook. Here's a recent headline: MONKS FIGHT ON ROOF OF HOLIEST PLACE—"Eleven monks were treated in hospital after a fight broke out for control of the roof of the Church of the Holy Sepulcher in Jerusalem." Could I make that up?

If I've remembered a dream, I'll write out what I can recall. I have far too many dreams of being at writers' conferences, and they are never about teaching or about stories. They're about trying to meet someone, anyone, at a restaurant. I'm always alone. I never find the person or the restaurant. No one else wants to hear my dreams. I suppose I could pay a shrink to listen, but I'd prefer to bring my anxiety to the page. Occasionally, a character winds up dreaming a dream a lot like mine.

I make notes about the novel or story I'm working on, and enter interesting facts, such as: "All Europeans descend from five females"; or curious behaviors, such as: "Chambermaid at the Hotel Gunther drinks water right out of the pitcher." I write them down because something about them intrigued me, and I don't know what it is or how I'll exploit them. My job is to jot.

Here's a magazine article about nanobes, the smallest form of terrestrial life—or are they? Here's a rather sad entry: "Not many years ago—during our summer travels, we actually signed up for the Super 8 Motel Discount Plan. Stay 'x' number of nights and get another night free."

I keep a list of possible titles, ("1-2-3 O'Leary"), and a list of names. Just now while writing, I got an e-mail from a woman in Panama City, Florida, inviting me to a writers' conference (no doubt I'll dream about it tonight—can't find the oyster bar). Her name? River Jordan. I wrote it down. I've got names of businesses. A B&B called The Cat Dragged Inn. I saw it out of a bus window somewhere between Stratford and London. When I was looking for the name of a beauty parlor while writing *Deep in the Shade of Paradise*, I read through the notebooks and found the one I used: "Pug Wolfe's Curl Up & Dye." Pug Wolfe is a real beautician in Cleveland, Mississippi. My friend, the poet Carolyn Elkins, gets her hair done at "Pug's New Generation Beauty Shop." I stole Pug's name. What I learned when the book came out was that Pug first wanted to call her shop "Curl Up & Dye," but her family vetoed the idea. Maybe now, she'll change it.

In my notebook, I also write down quotes on writing or on thinking. For example, Diane Arbus said, "I really believe there are things nobody would see if I didn't photograph them."

I keep lists of words that I want to use in my next novel: "carillonneur, cark, dogsbody [which my spell check just informed me is not a word—don't trust spell check and don't even install grammar check], brabble, hobbledehoy, scumble, skimble, frippet."

I write about my childhood, about, say, old Mike Thompson who owned the little market at the corner, and how he read the *Jewish Weekly* at the register and totaled up our purchases in pencil on the brown paper bag that we'd carry home. When I think of Mike, I remember Whitey, who lived behind the store and was convinced the FBI had his teeth wired so they could read his thoughts; and Vito, who wound up in a shootout with some Oklahoma police force; and Carl Brin, who shot his junior high school teacher and stole my basketball and my baseball glove. If you have your pen in hand, one thing leads to another.

I glue in cartoons—I love *Sylvia*, postcards—the Moses Motel in Monroe, Louisiana—who knows what character might check in; and photographs of possible settings for scenes. If I hear a line that I like, I write it down: "I stayed up all night with this chicken, and you're not going to eat it?" Or a situation: "A fundamentalist preacher is harassed and herded by a guy with a remote-control car."

I write out ideas for future stories or poems or plays. You get the idea—whatever I want to hold onto, I write down. Now I've got it, and don't need to be bothered with remembering it, and I can get on with the writing. When I write, I have the notebook on the desk for that which won't fit in the story I'm working on. And I keep a memo pad or index cards around to write down the intrusions from the real world—"Buy cream." "Call Jeffrey." "Type notes for class." I write them down and I forget them until I've finished writing. If I don't write them down, they nag at me, distract me from the work. Joan Didion says that note taking is done by those of us who were "afflicted apparently at birth with some presentiment of loss." That pretty much describes fiction writers.

Now that you've got the notebook, take it with you. Try writing in different places. (Before you do, gather up all those scattered notes you have and enter all of them in the notebook.) Try to write in at least one new place a week if you can. Carry a list of writing exercises with you at all times if you are worried about having nothing to write. Whenever you get a chance in your day to sit, write. Write in a bar. Not one of these franchise fern bars, but the neighborhood pub. A place where people go to talk. Listen to the patrons. Jot down what they're saying. That smell of cigarette smoke—how would you describe it? What does it remind you of? What are people wearing? What does that tell you about them? And at some point someone will ask you what you're doing, and you'll say you're a writer, and he'll tell you his story.

Write in a doctor's office. Who's there? Take a look at the magazine titles stacked on the coffee table. What mood does the place put you in? Write about that. Describe the sounds coming from beyond the pebbled glass window. What is unique about this doctor's office? How is it different from every other doctor's office in the world? Those folks waiting with you have stories. What do you imagine they are? Ask someone why they are there. Write about what happens.

Try writing in other places where people gather—cafés, malls, bus stops. If your characters drive expensive cars, then you might bring that notebook out to the country club and settle into the nineteenth hole. Write in a church, an old church if you can, a Catholic church if possible. Can you smell the incense? What is the effect of the light flooding through the stained glass? Write in a cemetery (a good source of names, by the way) or in a rowboat drifting on a pond. Write in an art museum. Write in a library. Libraries are great democratic institutions—we all show up there at one time or another. Write about the people you see and the books they are reading. Why is it that some people's voices carry across the room?

You're a writer now, and a writer writes. Any time, any place. That's his or her job. So take your tools with you wherever you go. The Muse is as likely to sit across the bar from you as to come by your office for a chat, and you want to be prepared when she taps your shoulder and says, "Look at the ladies at the next table." And you look over and see two elderly gals with face lifts, one of them telling the other about the Internet dating service she belongs to and about the loser she went out with the night before. "The first thing he said was, 'Do you own a car?' We went to Lolo's Chicken and Waffles for dinner, and he let me pay the tab. I told him, 'Have a nice life, Massimo.'" By now you ought to be writing as fast as you can. The stories are out there, but stories only happen to people who write them down.

Presidential elections. Right now a hospital is accusing labor organizers of using voodoo to frighten the workers into voting for union representation. And they're serious. The recent Miami police chief and city manager Donald Warshaw was arrested for stealing money from the "Do the Right Thing Foundation" so he could buy tickets to Marlins' games and nights out with his mistress. (Surreal postscript: in prison Warshaw taught classes to his fellow inmates. "Dress for Success," "Communication Technique," and "How to Find a Job.") Hialeah Mayor Raul Martinez has been indicted three times (but never convicted). In Hialeah Gardens, the miniskirt mayor was accused of hiring a hit man to kill her husband. She was convicted. Her husband testified on her behalf. Commissioner Humberto Hernandez went to jail for voter fraud. His wife was having an affair with his lawyer. He appealed his conviction. He also said, "If you've been here long enough, you know that nobody gives a flying fuck if you ran a clean campaign. Nobody gives a shit if you're involved in absentee ballot fraud or what have you. The bottom line is that you won." Crazy Joe Carollo and the X-man Xavier Suarez squared off in the Miami mayoral race, which Suarez apparently won until they tallied up the number of dead people who voted for him, some more than once. Suarez showed up in the middle of the night in his robe at a woman's house. He was carrying a gun and wanted to know why she didn't vote for him. Carollo (who redundantly vilified the INS agents who rescued [verb of choice] Elian as "atheists": "They don't believe in God.") was arrested for throwing a teapot at his wife in a domestic disturbance. He showed up at a news conference with a Catholic priest at his side. U.S. Attorney Kendall Coffey resigned from his job when he bit a stripper on the ass and charged a $900 bottle of champagne to his credit card and showed up later as lead attorney for Elian's family. (You can still see Kendall commenting as a legal expert on CNN and other news outlets— they apparently think he's a real lawyer and not the buffoon we know him to be.) City Commissioner Joe Gersten makes Kendall look virtuous. Joe reported his Mercedes stolen, but it turns out he'd leant it to his crack dealer and his prostitute friends. He fled to Australia where he's trying to get his license to practice law. At a County Commission meeting, Chairwoman Gwen Margolis tried to cut off Commissioner Natacha Seijas in the middle of a funding appeal. Seijas told Margolis, "You're going to leave in a body bag if you keep this up." Operation Clean Sweep turned up lots of crooked judges (surprise, surprise—we elect them!), one of whom offered to turn over info to the bad guys about a confidential informant—for $50,000.

Several of the 9/11 highjackers lived within two miles of my house and worked out up the street at the Dania Health Club. The head of the Broward County teachers' union was arrested for child pornography. There are currently five hundred children missing from the state's child welfare system. The governor hires a guy to take over the system, a guy who has written favorably on corporal punishment. It goes on and on.

MY OWN PARTICULAR CUSTOM

Reginald Gibbons

I looked through a journal of mine from several years ago to get a little distance on what I have written in this mode, and I noticed a few entries that would illustrate how my journal keeping feeds my writing of poetry and fiction, and my thinking about them, as well. Amid other jottings to which they were not related, the description of a pet crow and of a rainstorm in the entry of November 8, 1990, were the first germs of what became chapters of my novel, *Sweetbitter,* which I had begun nearly two years earlier, on January 1, 1988. I see the crow and rainstorm in my journal as hints of what was already moving in my memory and unconscious; my writing down these few words was not really my first attempt to begin to create a scene for the larger work, but rather a kind of marker buoy that I threw into the waters to remind me to go back and search the depths beneath it:

The weather was gathering, threatening rain. A thunderstorm had been building, far off to the west, and now it was going to fill the quiet night with its threats. A sizzling bolt of lightening burst out sideways above them, searing its thick knotted length on the dark sky for a long instant like an engorged vein on the very arm of God. She was blinking up where the flash had been. The immense darkness of the woods around them had turned in the moment of the bolt into a frightening innumerableness of detail and in that lit instant every leaf and twig, every thread of their clothes and hair on their heads, was counted and recorded. Then came the blasting thunder, pushing through their bodies as if they were nothing, and beyond them echoing away over half the world.

In memory and feeling, as yet unexplored by my conscious mind, either in pure thought or already in the wonderfully complex process of writing, lay these subjects that I sensed, on that day, were important to my novel. I didn't end up pouring rain down on my characters, only threatening to. At the same time, a fallen leaf I've described in my writing journal remains where it fell, not yet used for anything more in my writing.

A little quatrain I jotted down in January 1991 was the seed of something that took a long time to come fully into being, as my writing usually does, and finally became a poem called "White Beach" (collected in *Sparrow: New and Selected Poems*). The finished poem preserves only a few words from the dull, original quatrain; but a mood that struck me, or into which I fell, that the quatrain marked, again like a buoy, was at the heart of the poem. Later came a process of drafting and revision, but, without having written down these four lines, I would probably never have written the poem. I have the impression that this is the way many poets work.

When I was still an undergraduate student, I started intermittently keeping a journal that was partly an analytical diary of things that happened and sometimes a trying out of ideas about what I was reading and writing. I have kept writing both sorts of entries, all these years, and added fragments that are those floating markers of my unconscious, which become more frequent as the years go by.

I use notebooks that I carry with me nearly everywhere, and I make several different sorts of entries in them—from fragments and even single words and unusual (but not comic) rhyme pairs that I almost never use but that I like to discover, to long passages of essayistic complete sentences—almost as if written for different audiences, although these initial audiences are all within myself. I write irregularly about my own life events; I sort out my observations about others; anatomize my relationships with others; record occasionally a dream; I comment to myself on what I'm reading; I try to figure out what poetry is, or fiction; I wonder about what I'm writing and what sort of writer I am; I record anecdotes, observed moments among strangers, acquaintances and friends; I work out lines of thought about what I see happening around me in our common life as a society. I try to articulate my thoughts and feelings about American life, and especially life inside the American ideology created and sustained by media, politics, and religion. I write down notes for poems and stories. (I keep separate notebooks for those projects that have become well defined.) I hastily scrawl scraps of language and writing that feel like beginnings or endings or possibilities of poems or stories and that have arrived, finally, from their origins in my unconscious. I write down things I hear others say. I sketch (and use these sketches as bases of larger drawings).

I'm not able to write capsule character sketches like those at the heart of the diaries of Victor Klemperer, especially the portions written just before and during World War II; I don't record the course of larger events, although I wish I knew how to do so.

And from time to time—but not particularly often, because something about the reading of my own entries disturbs me, embarrasses me, makes me feel like an especially intrusive voyeur of my own life—I go back through the pages. I scan for, and recopy into a working notebook, the first drafts, the isolated phrases, sometimes a few words out of the middle of something else—live words with feeling and thought still pulsing in them even though the mood of the moment of writing has long since passed. Especially when the mood has passed. These are the tatters, bits, and shards I want to make more of, and sometimes I do, although only of a few.

A number of years ago I was very taken by the published journal of George Seferis (and I included some especially striking excerpts from it in my anthology, *The Poet's Work*). Seferis gave me permission to acknowledge feeling baffled or thwarted somehow, when the poem won't go forward—or anywhere—yet not losing hope of eventually finding a way to write what I could sense I wanted to write. Seferis encourages patience and a deep sense of the body as the source of symbolic thinking. He records anecdotes of experience as if to confirm or even shape his sense of poetry. I have also been moved by the power of Witold Gombrowicz's uncompromising and hard self-presentation and thinking in his diary, and also by the journals of Thoreau, Kafka, and Woolf. They are like black-and-white candid or news photos that seem to seize, out of what happens to happen, an inevitability of witness. The keeping of a journal is a peculiar form of writing practice; whether deliberate or hasty, formal or casual, whether more or less honest (depending on one's mood and motives), it seems not quite fully meant to be private, even at its most private.

Another value of reading back over a journal, as well as old poems or fiction, is that over time you can see patterns of feelings, perceptions of the world and the people in it, of thinking, that help bring your unconscious life into view. That level of my inner life is where the feelings and thoughts first arrive. For me, such inquiry into my own unconscious, however unavoidably incomplete, helps me to find my way toward writing that excites me, perhaps even to move deliberately beyond past obsessions, or at least move toward new ones. I have long believed Keats's assertion, and later restatements of it by other writers, that writing is self-making.

Another way of journal keeping is nicely described by Thomas Mann in the journal he kept in the 1930s, after the Nazis forced him from Germany and he lost all the routines and places that had been home to him. Having already won the Nobel Prize, having married money and made more of it, he was a materially cosseted public figure who enjoyed an esteem shared by only a handful of other writers, then or now—admired by great minds, always attended by well-wishers, expected to make public statements on politics as well as art, spending all his working time on his books and correspondence, with few, if any, of the practical daily duties and responsibilities, which were managed by his wife, Katia, and even by his daughter, Erika. Nevertheless, his diary is very matter-of-fact, and I hear a voice that is kindred to our ordinary ones in this passage that he wrote on Sunday, February 11, 1934:

> These diary notes, resumed in Arosa during days of illness brought on by inner turmoil and the loss of our accustomed structured life, have been a comfort and support up to now, and I will surely continue with them. I love this process by which each passing day is captured, not only its impressions, but also, at least by suggestion, its intellectual direction and content as well, less for the purpose of rereading and remembering than for taking stock, reviewing, maintaining awareness, achieving perspective. . . .

If I urge others to keep a journal for writing, I am only urging on them my own particular custom. Not only some writers, but also some politicians, sycophants, lovers of the powerful, torturers and victims, doctors and patients, bird-watchers, fly fisherman, dreamers, blessed lovers, and all sorts of other persons keep journals. The keeping in itself refines no virtue, enforces no honesty. But then personal honesty and virtue are not required of a writer, even though they can add immeasurably to what a person can accomplish as a writer. A writing journal is only a process by which one looks at life and a way with words and symbols, with the possibilities of image and story, or the unfolding of a sequence of rhythms and discoveries of feeling.

THOUGHTS ON A
WRITER'S JOURNAL

Rebecca McClanahan

Every day all over the world, writers station themselves at their desks and attempt to ask the hard questions. Then, for weeks, months, sometimes years afterward, they labor to shape artful texts from the difficult and unanswerable, the thing that, in the words of Samuel Butler, "refuses to go away." As any writer knows, this is hard work. Serious work. Not only must we locate our most urgent question, our deepest confusion, "the human heart in conflict with itself" (Faulkner's phrase), but we must also connect with our readers. Is it any wonder we become discouraged at the seemingly impossible task set before us?

This writer does, at least. If I'm lucky, sometimes the universe-in-the-form-of-the-Muse cooperates. The words click together, truth rears its ugly or beautiful head, and I find my way out. When this doesn't happen, when discouragement sets in, when I lose perspective, when I find that—yawn and yawn again—I am boring myself to death on the page, I reach for my journal. There, within its pages, I search for the authentic voice I lost somewhere along the way. Almost always it is there, hiding in some phrase I jotted down, half-asleep, one rainy morning. Or in a map or drawing I scribbled in its margins. Or in the unsent letter I drafted to some long forgotten self. Within the pages of my journal, no one is watching, judging, or assigning. There is no one to please. I don't have to finish what I start; I don't have to shape the words for other eyes to see. The writing can take any form—dream, rant, dialogue, confession, joke, anecdote—or no form at all. Yes, life is deadly serious, and sometimes writing is too. But in my journal, another life is possible. Many other lives. Here are a few of the lives that, over the past forty-plus years, my journal has lived.

Compost Bin

Years ago, when a book reviewer sent an e-mail to help prepare me for an interview, his final question captured my attention: "What is your theory of composting?" Before he could discover and correct the typographical error, my mind had already left on its own journey: *Composting.* Isn't it strange that only one letter separates two words, two worlds? A gardener saves everything organic—apple peelings, leaves, eggshells, coffee grounds—allows the mixture to breed a while, rot a while; turns it occasionally with a pitchfork, stirring up stored heat; and, finally, works the rich mulch into the depleted soil, where new crops sprout the following spring. Isn't that, in effect, what I do when I write? Into my journal, a.k.a. compost heap, I toss scraps of organic matter that come my way—daily wonderings, newspaper clippings, quotations, drafts of poems and stories, sketches, dream records, song lyrics, jokes, weather reports, the mundane details of my personal life—trusting that they will be useful, that the scraps of my daily life will enrich the soil from which new poems, stories, and essays will sprout.

So, yesterday, having snagged a free ticket for a rehearsal of the New York Philharmonic's gala opening and spending one delicious hour in the presence of a master cellist who exuded more joy than I've witnessed for months in my beloved city, I scribbled on the back of the program a few words that I later copied into my journal: "Yo-Yo Ma Loves Yo Ma-Ma." I liked the way the words turned in on each other, the mirroring effect. No deep insight, I realize. As it stands now, the phrase amounts to little more than a lame bumper sticker. Still, I know from experience that the phrase may lead to something. (Say, if Yo-Yo loves yo mama, he might love my mama as well, if he could just meet her.) A seed for a short story? Who knows. The scenario just might go somewhere. So I toss it onto the compost bin that is my journal.

Witness Stand

"Never write down anything you wouldn't want to be used in court," a lawyer friend once told me. I understand her reasoning, but it doesn't keep me from writing down plenty of things that might someday be used against me. I blame Great-Aunt Bessie. On my tenth birthday, she gave

me a pink, vinyl-covered diary with a tiny lock and key. I'd never thought
of words as secrets I could lock away, and the newfound power was exhilarating. If I had the only key, no one else could read what I'd written—
not my parents, teachers, friends, or, most important, my siblings. I could
write whatever I wanted and no one would know. I could scribble, mis-
spell words right and left, even tell lies without getting caught.

Not that I wanted to lie. What I wanted was to tell what the witnesses
on *Perry Mason* promised to tell: the whole truth and nothing but. The
whole truth, I'd discovered, was often hard to say, especially to other people. "If you can't say something nice, don't say anything at all," my first-
grade teacher had admonished. That kept me quiet for a long time. But
once I opened the diary and started writing, the truth came spilling out.
This still happens to me when I open my journal, for something about a
journal's pages encourages truth telling. I write quickly, before I lose my
nerve. "The truth is I envy C's life. I'm afraid to say that I'm lonely. The
truth is I'm getting old, my eyelids are drooping, my poems are. . . ."

As I write, I don't censor the many contradictions, dichotomies, and
illogical statements, for truth always has more than one side and rarely
follows the rules of logic. "I love New York and hate New York." "The
old woman's breasts were shrunken and beautiful." "Money is the most
stupid and important thing in our lives." "I wanted to kiss him and
never see him again." Sometimes I write about the worst things I can
imagine happening—to me, to my family and friends. Terrible things.
Unspeakable. Except on the journal page. On the journal page, nothing
is unspeakable. I can tell the whole truth and nothing but and no one
will be harmed. The worst that can happen—which usually turns out to
be the best that can happen—is that for a moment my inner world splits
open, shattering old notions, white lies, and misconceptions, a process
which may lead to public truth-telling on the page, the kind of truth-
telling I struggle to bring forth in my poems and essays, but not until
I'm good and ready. Not until I've talked it through in the pages of my
journal.

Playroom

As I said earlier, the world outside our door is, for the most part, deadly
serious. Grown-ups are expected to act in a grown-up fashion. We are
supposed to pay our bills, mow our lawns, go to our jobs, and balance our

checkbooks. Sometimes, without intending to, I carry this nose-to-the-grindstone mentality into my writing room: I must write about important issues and not waste time on frivolity. My writing must be a tool for self-improvement; it must teach me something. No doodling in the margins, no playful Saturday afternoons making up songs about three-toed tree toads.

When I lose the joy of writing for writing's sake, I return to my journal. Within its covers I can play like a child, record the silliest, goofiest ideas that occur to me: "(Motto for taxidermist) Forever Yours: The Look of Life Without the Trouble." "Embroidery is crewel and unusual punishment." "Nature isn't the only mother who abhors a vacuum." I can turn a page and sketch a cartoon. In one, a nursing baby is singing, "Thanks for the mammaries." In another, a man is wearing not a checkered past but a plaid one.

I know, I know. I should definitely keep my day job. But who knows? Maybe someday I'll write a story about a character who goes around saying goofy things. Stranger things have happened. One of my cartoons—of a dime walking disdainfully past a penny lying in the gutter—evolved into a poem about the invention of zero. You just never know. Besides, it's fun to play, and sometimes the simple act of playing with words and phrases is enough to start the literary juices flowing. "Say it again," my nephew begs. So I bring Lewis Carroll's poem out of mothballs: "'Twas brillig, and the slithy toves / Did gyre and gimble in the wake." Then, I open my journal and begin making lists of wonderful sounding words, the kind of words that, as a young student once described it to me, "feel good to my ears": *blub, lurk, aubergine, Nefertiti.*

Many writers keep word lists, or play with word combinations as they write. Roy Blount Jr.'s published journals contain fascinating sets of word pairs: *lacy pants / participants; baseline / Vaseline, wrapper / reappear.* Serious poets, too, attest to the power of wordplay: "I found these words and put them together," wrote William Stafford, "by their appetites and respect for each other." Yes, some words simply want to live together; others have strong family likenesses. These, for instance, that I recently jotted down in my journal: *confetti, graffiti, cherry tree.* If I keep playing long enough, the skeleton of a poem might emerge:

> From the cherry tree, blossoms
> scatter like confetti

onto the curb, against
the graffiti.

Sometimes I uncover words hidden within other words. I recently discovered *marriage* tucked inside *miscarriage,* which started me thinking . . . *then comes marriage, then carriage, miscarriage, miscarriage of justice, justice of the peace.* Sometimes journal play is like a game of leapfrog, the mind hopping from one image to another, one idea to another, surprising us with connections we had not known were there. And isn't that what writing is all about—discovering something new? If we can't surprise ourselves on the page, we will never surprise our readers.

Writing Workshop

The freedom to write whatever we want, in whatever form we wish, is one of the many benefits of journal writing. But absolute freedom can tyrannize as well as liberate. To invent a world where anything is possible, even the world of your own writing, requires great stores of creative energy. Sometimes, when faced with unlimited possibilities, I become overwhelmed, unable to write the first word, or, after writing for a while, I feel I've exhausted what I have to say. Like a child at the end of summer who longs for anything—yes, even school—that will provide structure for his days, I begin longing for writing assignments, deadlines, even periodical progress reports to keep me going. Quite often, editors or peers provide the necessary structure, but my journal is also a valuable workshop tool. Within its pages, I can be student, teacher, coach, mentor, editor, and peer. I can assign and complete writing exercises, set deadlines, and even critique my works-in-progress. A recent list of self-made assignments includes:

Stories about the cars in my life and the places they took me
A book of interrelated poems about Central Park
An essay called "I'm Nobody, Who Are You?"

Giving myself assignments helps jump-start my writing on days when my mind is stalled; it also focuses random daytime thoughts and even nighttime dreams. Recording an assignment in my journal is like addressing a postcard to myself and dropping it into the mailbox of my unconscious. Once the assignment is given, my mind starts looking for ways to complete it. Even when my conscious mind forgets I ever made the assignment, my unconscious mind remembers, the way it remembered to buy chicken broth and celery today even though I left the grocery list at home. When my mind is blank, when I can think of nothing at all to write, I borrow an assignment someone else has devised, copy the assignment into my journal, and then complete it as I would an assignment given by a teacher.

Leaping off from someone else's thoughts is another way I discover potential assignments. My journal is filled with quotations taken from newspapers, books, radio and television, bumper stickers, lists of rules and regulations, overheard conversations—whatever strikes my interest. I sometimes find gems in unexpected places. Once, while leading a fourth-grade poetry lesson, I saw written on a child's paper, "The truth is sticky, babe." I jotted it in my journal, forgot about it and then rediscovered it a year or two later while I was struggling with a poem about the difficulty of escaping our personal histories. The child's insight about the stickiness of truth helped me locate the central image in my poem, and I ended up using her quotation as the poem's epigraph (giving her credit, of course).

Quotations can lead to all sorts of writing experiences. You can illustrate a quotation with a personal event, question the assumption beneath a quotation, argue with it, or write from the point of view of its real or imagined author. I've written several first-person monologues in which I imagine the thoughts and experiences of real-life people and fictional characters based on quotations I recorded in my journal: Peter Pan's Wendy, a clay-eater, my dead grandmother, an unborn child, and others. I recently discovered the Spanish proverb "More things grow in the garden than the gardener sows," which made me remember a Barbie doll I once found buried in my tulip bed. I had forgotten about the doll, but now I sense a story growing from the experience. How did the doll get there? Who buried it, and why?

Posing questions is another way to create writing assignments. My journal is filled with questions, from trivial to serious and everything in-between: "Why am I so drawn to bald men?" "Why am I terrified of tunnels?" "If the cyst is malignant, will I choose chemo or surgery?" "Why do I paint my toenails red?" Any of these questions could suggest a story, poem, song, or letter I could write.

Sometimes I use my journal to assign deadlines: By Friday, I'll finish the first draft of the sonnet; by next Tuesday, I'll revise the story about my brother. Giving myself deadlines not only increases my chances of completing projects; it also keeps me from judging my early efforts too harshly. After all, if I have only a week to draft the essay, I can't expect it to be a magnum opus, right? But when it comes time to test revised drafts, the stakes are higher, and I often talk to myself on the journal's pages, providing the kind of feedback a peer or editor might provide. I check myself with questions: "Is this line too sentimental?" "Have I resisted the easy answer?" "Is there a better way to say this while still remaining true to the experience?" Sometimes I push myself to work harder; other times I comfort myself by recalling past difficulties that ended in success; sometimes I simply write through a literary problem until I reach a new understanding.

Life Record

Both *diary* and *journal* are rooted in the Latin for *day*, and the first journals were day-by-day renderings of events and transactions. Clerks documented court proceedings, sailors updated logbooks, private citizens recorded their daily comings and goings. William Saroyan, who kept a diary for many years, noted that the journal keeper "is obsessed by the wish to know what happened, and the only way he can ever hope to know is to have the written daily account to consult at his convenience. Otherwise it is all forgotten." Saroyan's statement may appear old-fashioned, even stodgy, to those who view the journal primarily as a tool for expressing emotions. However, though daily accounts of what happened don't appeal to everyone, the benefits of keeping such accounts are many. First, as Saroyan mentions, a journal helps jog our memories of past events, the places and people we have known. Second, a journal encourages regular appointments with the desk and provides an orderly place to store the chaotic pieces of our lives. Third, journal keeping prompts us to notice the extraordinary detail in even the most ordinary day.

Finally, if we later choose to share our journals, or if our descendants choose to, the journals will serve as records of particular places and times. When we read the diaries of Samuel Pepys, Fanny Burney, or Sei Shonagon, we're treated to a cultural and historical education more lively than any textbook account. Even the most casual, nonliterary record can open windows into personal and public histories.

My grandmother kept a shorthand diary by jotting notes on her kitchen calendar: "butter and cream for Sisson's," "three chicks pipped today," "macaroni for Grange supper." Her sister, Great-Aunt Bessie, kept more detailed observations of daily events—trips taken, books read, rare birds sighted, and the external and internal weather of her days. Reading her diaries, I learn from the inside out how it felt to be a teenager in the 1890s, a farmer and Red Cross volunteer during World War I, and a widow who traveled the country by Greyhound bus during the 1950s: "I've soaked my corns in both the Atlantic and the Pacific," she wrote.

A diary rooted in daily detail is a double gift to its reader. When we read someone else's journal or reread our own, we learn not only about the person who recorded these particular details but also about the outer world in which the author moved. "No man is an island," wrote John Donne; no woman is either. We breathe and move on a continent larger than the self, and the landscape of that continent shapes us. The stories of our lives are also the stories of the towns we've visited, the people we've known, the books we've read, the clothes we've bought, the vaccinations we've received, the cats and dogs we've named and buried, the meals we've prepared and eaten. Keeping a record of our comings and goings reminds us that our lives are continuing sagas unfolding, in specific detail, day after particular day.

Confession Booth

"Dear Kitty," begins Anne Frank's diary, "I hope I will be able to confide everything to you, as I have never been able to confide in anyone, and I hope you will be a great source of comfort and support." Even if we don't address our diary or journal by name, when we commit personal thoughts to the page, we are in effect constructing another self with whom to share intimate confidences. The phrases associated with journal writing suggest this intimacy. When we *make an entry* in a diary or journal, we enter it as we might enter a secret room, a guarded conversation, or a lover's bed; and keeping a journal is not only an act of care and guardianship but also one of personal possession. We are possessive of our innermost thoughts. We don't want just anyone listening in. Not that we don't have friends, spouses, lovers, therapists, priests, or pets in whom to confide. (Many cats, I've discovered, make excellent listeners.) But there is nothing like the intimacy that occurs within the journal's pages. The page never yawns, interrupts, or walks away with its tail in the air. It just listens.

Sometimes we whisper secrets. The journal leans close and attends to each word. It will never betray our confidence. Its lips are sealed.

Sometimes we rant and rave, flail and pound against the journal's pages; we curse our lives and everyone in it. The journal is our punching bag, our padded cell. It absorbs the blows.

Sometimes we confess. We enter the booth, and the journal lifts the partition. No matter if it's been three weeks since our last confession, or three years. The journal welcomes us home.

When we whine like a spoiled brat, the journal simply leans back, folds its arms across its chest, and nods. It doesn't tell us to stop acting like a child. And when we make no sense, when one phrase tangles in the next and we can't untie the knot, the journal is patient. It's not going anywhere. It's got all the time in the world. Besides, a journal knows our history as well as we do, sometimes even better. Because it has recorded each confidence, it can recall our past and, in so doing, help us imagine the future. This too will pass, it seems to say. Like a longtime partner who knows us well enough to finish our sentences or fill in the blanks when we're searching for a word, a journal can fill the awkward silences. When we are voiceless, it helps us find our voice again. Sometimes the voice we find is strange or otherworldly, singing in an unknown key. We dream dreams and see visions. Our daylight self tells us these dreams are crazy, impractical, impossible to achieve, so why even bother? The journal says, "Tell me more."

FROM WRITER'S NOTEBOOK
TO POETIC JOURNAL

Mark Pawlak

I learned from Denise Levertov, my first poetry teacher, the value of keeping a journal, something she did regularly as a way of inviting the Muse. Actually, she kept two kinds of journals, and she encouraged her students to follow her example. One was a writer's notebook—a place to jot down lines from important poems or passages that expanded or deepened your understanding of poetry. If a word, phrase, or image came to us, she encouraged us to write it down in our notebooks; also snippets of conversation and observations of people and objects.

The other kind of journal Levertov kept was a dream journal. As an enthusiastic reader of Carl Jung, Levertov placed a lot of emphasis on the importance of dreams. She believed they were worth recording and that once written in the notebooks might become the seeds from which poems could sprout. She once shared an example of a fragment of one of her own dreams that she had recorded about a sandal with a broken thong, which later resulted in a poem ("The Broken Sandal").

I took Levertov's advice. Keeping a writer's notebook is something I began back then, so many years ago when I first started out as a poet. I have had one ever since. From time to time, I have also kept a dream journal. My notebooks have been the place where my own ideas about poetry have evolved, as well as where many of my own poems have gotten their start.

I used my practice of journaling when working on my first poetry collection, *The Buffalo Sequence.* The poems document my efforts to retrieve the memories of my childhood, growing up in the working-class Polish neighborhoods of Buffalo, New York. It was also an attempt to recover the colorful language and ethnic speech patterns that had been educated out of me as I followed the path to become a fully assimilated, college-educated American. At the time of composing those poems, I carried on an active correspondence with friends and relatives back in Buffalo, often recording in my notebook stories, images, and phrases copied out of their letters.

The following poem from *The Buffalo Sequence* is an imaginative para-phrase of my mother's letters, in which she always spoke of herself in the third person. The first draft was written in my notebook:

> [Dear . . .]
> Today there is no letter from her boys
> and her son's mother is sad.
> Her son's father is sad too
> —they know how he misses his boys;
> and couldn't they show a little more appreciation?
> Today when there is no word,
> she is watching her husband in his uneasy rest.
> He has finished dinner and now
> stretches his skin, rough from hard work,
> wall to wall on the living room floor.
> The noise his belly makes,
> she is certain,
> he must be digesting over and over
> the meal stewed once again
> with the bones of happier days.
> Her sons know their father is a good man.
> If there is any place not full in his belly now
> it is where he keeps a vacancy,
> anytime, for his boys.
> And couldn't they show a little more appreciation?
> Last night, her husband did not sleep
> but tossed and tossed. . . .
> When he pulled the sheets over his head
> she thought it was the dark wave
> that one forgets under, forever.
> She worries about that good man.
> Recently, his liver has been remembering

his wild younger days
—before her son's mother knew him;
her husband is getting old and she worries . . .
Her sons know their father never complains.
She could tell,
his great arched rib ached him
when he came home from work today,
the one he stretches from horizon to horizon
to keep back the darkness for his boys.
Her sons really could show a little more appreciation.
[Mother]

This habit of keeping a writer's notebook gained additional value for me when the time came to trade in my young poet, Bohemian lifestyle for the responsibilities of husband and parent, which included holding down a regular job. It became my way of keeping in touch with my poet-self whenever the demands of teaching, college administration, and editing a magazine interfered with writing poems on a regular basis and also kept me from reading poetry for my own pleasure for days or weeks at a time. My notebook, besides being a connection to my interior self and a way of perceiving the world, was a place for me to work out my ideas about poetry, and a place to chart the evolution of my own work and where it was headed. On those pages I wrote down passages from other poets, and from writers about craft, as well as their thoughts about what constituted poetry.

My notebook became a workbook for fleshing out my own poetics, building on the ideas and practice of others. At that time, I was a devoted reader of Henry David Thoreau's journals. When I learned that he had copied out and rearranged pieces from them thematically to construct his justly famous essays and *Walden,* I became inspired to mine the material from my own notebooks and organize it. This approach led me to write several essays on poetry, editing, class, and ethnicity.

The example below is my journal entry in response to something poet David Ignatow once said in an interview that is included in his book of essays and interviews, *Open between Us,* edited by Ralph J. Mills.

Excerpt from 1983:

The question, what makes a "found poem" a poem, is essentially the same question as was once asked about the "free verse" poem and, more recently, about the "prose poem." The answer is essentially the same. "It's vision that counts." That's how David Ignatow put it. "Anything that's held together by an insight, around which everything gathers and goes towards and helps build—that is a poem."

I later returned to my notebook where I reflected at some length on this idea of vision as the organizing principle for poems, and I linked it with other statements about poetry that I'd copied out by Tristan Tzara and Marcel Duchamp. Eventually, I combined all these with descriptions of my habit of working with found language in my own poems. The result was the essay on found poetry, "Machines Made of Words," that appeared in the literary magazine *Object Lesson*. The habit of keeping a journal helped me collect ideas and work out the essay's outline.

Starting about ten years ago, something new happened in my notebooks that coincided with spending a few weeks each summer with my family in a rented cottage on the coast of Maine. My entries began to include things noticed from the porch overlooking Tenant's Harbor where I sat reading early each morning, or while strolling the rocky shores, or touring the surrounding area by car on rainy days. Observations about lobstermen and their boats, about the varieties of luxury yachts at anchor, about the flora and fauna of the area, about the local residents and their habits filled the pages, as did place names, fragments of overheard conversations, and words and phrases found on signs, on restaurant placemats, and in the regional newspapers.

Soon the variety of entries in my notebooks rivaled the thirteenth-century Japanese *Pillow Book* of Sei Shonagon. This change in the content of my writer's notebook eventually resulted in "Hart's Neck Haibun," a lengthy, five-part poetic journal that makes up the backbone of my latest poetry collection, *Official Versions* (2006). Haibun is a Japanese poetic form dating back many centuries that alternates prose passages with haiku poems. The most famous example is Basho's *Narrow Road to the Deep North and Other Travel Sketches,* his travel journal written as haibun. I adopted the form because it was roughly analogous to my Maine journals.

The poetic journal / haibun became the primary mode of writing for me, one that I valued in itself and not just as a workbook for ideas that would later find their way into crafted essays or discrete poems. My new regard for the material that filled my notebook pages soon echoed

Thoreau's, who privileged his journals over his other writing, because they were more spontaneous and closer to his lived life.

Here is an excerpt from *Journals of Henry David Thoreau* written on January 27, 1852:

> Thoughts written down thus in a journal might be printed in the same form with greater advantage than if the related ones were brought together in separate essays. They are now allied to life, and are seen by the reader not far-fetched. It is more simple, less artful.

In other words, like Thoreau, I began to see the poetic journal as a distinct genre, different from my writer's notebook. Analogous to Thoreau's journals, are artists' sketchbooks and their relation to finished paintings. Traditionally, the sketchbook was used in the field to record quick impressions later to be fully worked up in the studio into large paintings in oils on stretched canvases; but some artists came to see their plein air sketches on paper, bound in notebooks, done in pencil, pastel crayon, or watercolors, as finished works in themselves. In the end, journaling is a question of intention—whether the journal is a private record not meant for publication, an artifact, or written with publication in mind.

Keeping a journal of observational poems is no longer only what I do during summer vacations. It has now become a regular mode of working for me—putting down words, sometimes in lines, sometimes in sentences, daily, or nearly daily in spiral-bound six-by-four-inch notebooks that I carry with me at all times.

Since studying with Denise Levertov, I realize that the poetic journal is a literary genre, distinct from the journal as workbook. Unlike what I learned from Levertov's insistence on keeping a writer's notebook, this was a lesson I absorbed through osmosis, by being in her presence, rather than through her conscious instruction. In the late sixties and early seventies, she brought to our class new installments pulled fresh from her typewriter of a poetic journal-in-progress that she had begun the year before. She invited us to read and discuss them, offer comments and suggestions in the same way we did with one another's work.

Reading her journal poems was a revelation, coming as they did right after a class on *The Waste Land* (not taught be Levertov) where the focus was Eliot's ideas about poems as carefully worked texts, steeped in classical literary references. Levertov, in contrast, demonstrated by example that effective poems could just as well be fresh and spontaneous as one's response to the day's events. They could be about what you were feeling at the moment, or about things you had just observed or recently contemplated.

Published journals and daybooks were commonplace in the sixties and seventies. A number of them were written by Levertov's contemporaries, including fellow "New" American poets Allen Ginsberg, Gary Snyder, Robert Creeley, Paul Blackburn, Philip Whalen, John Weiners, and Joanne Kyger. What made Levertov's poetic journal different was her conscious attempt to give shape and structure to it. The result is a push and pull between viewing the whole, as she indicates in her preface of *To Stay Alive*, "as table or chair with the requisite number of legs so as not to wobble"—a definition of poetic craft that Levertov borrowed from Ezra Pound—versus the poem as "a record of one person's inner / outer experience of America during the sixties and beginning of the seventies."

Levertov's "notebook" poem is an invaluable model that I will continue to look to for the answer to these questions as my own work in this genre continues to evolve. My instinct tells me that the journal poem or poem as journal needs to allow for some wobble; but wobble of a kind that, although eccentric like a top's, nevertheless follows a pattern around a center of balance.

THE ICEBREAKER

Lori Van Pelt

When I was a freshman in high school, our English teacher gave us an assignment to keep a journal. We were free to write about anything we wanted, and she promised she would not read our meanderings. The only catch was that we had to fill a certain number of pages each day. Our grade would be based not on our topics, but on our production.

She thus taught two lessons: how to write without inhibitions and how to produce pages on a regular schedule. Granted, when we were pressed for time, she saw journal entries composed in extra-large cursive with every other line left blank as we hurried to generate the designated number of pages by the end of the week. That formidable deadline loomed, and if we did not turn something in, we failed.

After that class, I did not keep a structured journal. On occasion, I wrote stuffy "Dear Diary" entries that were stilted and sporadic at best. Following graduation, I studied music and business and then took a job in a bank, leaving little time for journal writing. However, I did continue to write. In junior college, my poems were published in a literary magazine. While working at the bank, I penned features for the local newspaper. When I moved to a new town to complete my bachelor's degree in finance, I wrote a few articles for the campus newspaper and the alumni magazine. Journaling was once again relegated to the irregular entry, usually when I felt confused or elated about something.

Fortune smiled upon my graduation. Not only did a handsome and smart fiancé arrive on the scene, but also an intriguing full-time newspaper job in his hometown became available. "Serious" writing came to the forefront, and journaling halted. After about a year, I found that I enjoyed writing enough to try freelancing. Not long after, I discovered Julia Cameron's book *The Artist's Way*. She advocated writing "Morning Pages," a practice I've adhered to for the past decade. This informal journaling, three pages of early morning longhand, continues to be rewarding.

I use a simple spiral-bound, college-lined notebook, writing whatever comes to mind. I write as soon after I awaken from sleep as possible, and I do not stop to think about the way I'm writing. My pens vary, although my hand feels most comfortable with a felt-tip or gel-ink pen. Sometimes, I sharpen a pencil or two and scribble away.

The only restrictions are that I must write fast, keep my hand moving, and not cross anything out. If my internal editor scowls at an "incorrect" word or phrase, I simply follow that by writing whatever the "proper" word is and enclosing the right answer in parentheses. Then I continue. For example, a recent entry involved the tree I see outside my writing-room window. "I love that stately old cottonwood tree. It looks like a stalk of broccoli with a flowered head."

These pages are for my eyes only. Sometimes I jot a paragraph and skip a line before beginning the next paragraph. Sometimes the pages are easily filled. Anything goes here. To-do lists, wish lists, shopping lists, lists of five beautiful things I've seen recently, and lists of blessings to count might be interspersed with several sentences about my experiences on the day before. Complaints are also common.

I do not reread what I've written until several weeks later. At that time, I review my pages, underline good ideas and phrases and copy them in an idea file. In addition to being helpful for my writing, these pages are also therapeutic because I can see what issues have bothered me during the previous six or eight weeks. Those are the ones I revisit again and again. When I notice a pattern of negativity, I seek solutions. What actions can I take to alleviate this problem? Is it something petty and whiny that I need to drop? Sometimes, my problems are actually solved while writing. I might pose a question in my morning pages and have the answer right at hand as my pen moves across the page.

Although I'm not striving to write three pages of great prose every day, quite often ideas for stories, poems, and articles flow into my morning pages. *Flow* is the key word. My main objective for doing morning pages is priming the pump and stimulating my writing. Touching pen to page in the early morning with a preset goal breaks the ice of the blank page. My thoughts may be disjointed, ranging from "It's sunny but cold today. I miss my dad and wish he could be here to give me his advice" to "I don't have anything to write about today, and maybe I should just go get a real job." Most days, however, I enjoy writing these pages, and the mere act of writing them often sends me to my current project with greater energy and enthusiasm.

This increased zeal proved helpful when I worked on my book *Amelia Earhart: The Sky's No Limit,* one of the premier titles in Forge Publishing's American Heroes biography series. Faced with a tight deadline, I tried to compose one chapter each week while still writing morning pages. Doubts assailed me. There was so much information available about the famed aviatrix. What specifics should I include? How could I condense so much research into a fascinating read? After all that had been written about Amelia before, how could I write something fresh? How would I ever meet the deadline?

I surmounted these fears by turning to the page. Whenever I felt afraid, I wrote longhand in a separate spiral notebook. Rather than scribbling whatever came to mind, I jotted specifics about Amelia and the book. I combined my journalism training with my morning pages practice, asking myself the pertinent "who-what-where-when-why-and-how" questions and further focusing my thoughts by limiting this "interview" to each chapter. What events were occurring in Amelia's life at that time? What was going on in the rest of the world at that time? What was the main objective of the chapter? Who were the people involved? Where was Amelia? What was she doing? Why were these topics important? Could I just write three longhand pages answering these questions? Happily, yes, and frequently even more. This "idea journal" demolished the deep freeze of my fears and helped clarify my thoughts. Often while writing down the answers to these questions, I glided into real prose and began composing sections of the chapter.

When my editor, Dale L. Walker, suggested using a single word for the title of each chapter, it helped me think even more clearly. "Tomboy" guided me through Amelia's childhood, and "Turbulence" illustrated a particularly rough period of her life as well as one of her risky transoceanic flights. In the way that pilots take test flights to evaluate the performance of a new aircraft, my idea journal became a testing ground for ideas to take flight. In my case, however, intense scrutiny of the details would come later. Whatever I wrote down was okay because I could "fix" it later. The purpose of the journal was to provide a private space where I could write anything that occurred to me with regard to the task at hand. I was not risking editorial judgment but letting my writer glory in the joy of the journey. This journal allowed me to "fix" my thoughts before I affixed them to the prose of the chapter I was writing.

As my crafting the book progressed to Amelia's disappearance and the abundant theories about what happened to her, I found myself slowing down. Throughout the process, I came to know Amelia well and considered her a mentor. Among many other notable achievements, she flew solo across the Atlantic Ocean in her single-engine Vega and later wrote, "Everyone has his own Atlantics to fly. Whatever you want very much to do, against the opposition of tradition, neighborhood opinion, and so-called 'common sense,'—that is an Atlantic."

She did not mention the opposition of an internal editor, but these few words helped me cross the sea of pages necessary to completing her biography. By the time I reached the epilogue, I was paradoxically working at what felt like a snail's pace because I had enjoyed writing so much that I did not want to stop. In addition, I did not want to "close the book" on my relationship with Amelia Earhart. As a result, her quote about each of us having her own Atlantic to fly appeared often in my morning pages and still pops up when I face writing challenges.

Although I keep the idea journal, I do destroy my morning pages after I've reviewed them. They are private pages, after all, and by shredding them, I am keeping my bargain with my writer that they will not be seen by anyone else.

The idea-journal method helps with fiction as well. When writing my collection of short fiction, *Pecker's Revenge and Other Stories from the Frontier's Edge,* I kept notes for each story in a separate file folder. To distinguish these notes from my morning pages, I switched to 8 ½-by-11 yellow legal pads. I "assigned" myself three longhand pages of free-writing about the story. When creating fiction, as with my morning writing, I must write quickly, keep my hand moving across the page, and disallow crossouts.

Sometimes this free-write is entirely about a character. Sometimes dialogue comes. Sometimes a scene suggests itself. I write until the information dwindles. Many times, the words come so quickly that I write six or more pages. To keep my mind fluidly working on the story, I usually jot down a question or an idea that I'd like to write about the next day. This provides a starting point for approaching my task. These pages often ramble and go off on tangents, but after a few sessions, I know my characters well. Sometimes, the entire story is there, and sometimes I just have a glimmer of an idea. It doesn't matter. I'm only playing around on the page trying to fill the three-page quota as rapidly as possible. When I feel I can no longer write this way, I turn to my computer and start typing what I've written. On occasion, the story practically writes itself and I don't have much polishing or editing to do. More often, though, I find myself simply typing what I've already written longhand. When I have the horrid first draft with huge gaps and rare transitions entered on the computer, I print the pages. At that point, I can usually "see" how the story goes and move forward.

Again, pen in hand, I read what I've written and start jotting down whatever comes to mind. When the words begin to flow, my cursive spills across the bottom of the page and onto the back, and even onto blank yellow legal sheets. This is not at all neat but it doesn't matter. This is not for publication, after all, but for me. And hey, I really like that first paragraph of sharp dialogue. That's got great conflict. What if . . . ? You get the picture. This technique would not work for everyone, of course. But from my daily practice of morning pages, I have learned to break the ice on any writing project by taking pen in hand and simply writing down whatever comes to mind. By allowing myself the freedom to generate ideas and get my thoughts on paper without worrying about my internal editor, my actual editor, or the response of readers, I compose myself on the page. In the process, I discover the composition that is trying to get written. In this way, I've written two unpublished novels as well as numerous published works, including the Earhart biography, two nonfiction books of Wyoming profiles, two short-fiction collections, several short stories, magazine and newspaper articles, and even a few poems.

My words have spilled onto the frosty blank page each time through lessons learned years ago and followed today. All because of that simple high school assignment to keep a daily journal and an English teacher's pledge to let that writing remain private.

Part 5

THE JOURNAL FOR LIFE

"The diary deals always with the immediate present, the warm, the near, being written at white heat develops a love of the living moment. One thing is very clear—that both diary and fiction tend toward the same goal: intimate contact with people, with experiences, with life itself."

Anaïs Nin

DAILY DOODLES

Dorianne Laux

Journaling. All the time. Write, write, write. When did it start—this obsession—this "always have your head in a damn book, get down off your high horse, empty the trash, get up, get some EXERCISE." That's my father's voice. My mother secretly loves it, lets me read and write any time I want, doesn't even get mad when I write along the edges of her sheet music or between the black notes and the lyrics, just to see the words I've read and loved and memorized from her bookshelves: "Whose words are these . . . When the world is mud-luscious . . . I AM the people—the mob-the crowd-the mass . . ." spill from my own pencil like music onto the page.

The other day I was looking in her old English to French dictionary and saw one of my childhood scribbles on the *S* page: scribe: pointe à tracer. I was a tracer of words living on the point of a pen. I must have been three or four, and the scrawl is illegible, it could have been my first attempt at a letter or a snake. Already I saw the connection between books and writing, symbols and pictures, already I wanted to add my two cents. Write it. Write it down. Use every inch of available space.

My first real journals were my blue, ruled, school notebooks. God, how I loved those wide lines, the infinitude of pages, soon to be illegible. I wrote about my boyfriends, of course, but also about injustice. Oh, how I loathed injustice. "Death to injustice" was an actual sentence I once wrote. "I can hear America singing." I dared to write, "I can hear America sighing and breathing, dying and cleaving."

I wrote in the backseat of the car on family vacations, feeling an immense sorrow overwhelm me as I watched the strawberry pickers bent over between the tessellating rows. I wrote odes to their toast-brown arms and shining black hair, the men's white shirts stuck to their backs, the women in piñata-colored skirts tied in knots above their knees, the children in shorts and flip flops peeing yellow arcs into the dirt beneath the vines. And sluicing near them, above ground, irrigation water wheels— the prisms they made against the sky. And the slatted wooden boxes piled high with plucked fruit bound for picnic tables all across America.

I wrote and wrote and then threw the messy pages in the trash, tore the paper into smaller and smaller pieces so no one could read it. And when I didn't have a journal, I wrote on napkins, bathroom stalls, toilet paper, my palm, the insides of my arms, lunch bags, the white side of cigarette package foil, my birth certificate, my divorce settlement, telephone bills and the envelopes they arrived in, the edges of newspaper, receipts, and once, when walking through a forest, on the undersides of fallen leaves.

Hypergraphia. I was compelled to write, maybe because I wasn't allowed to speak. (I was four or five. My father was physically and sexually abusive, and the family lived in constant fear of him. My sister and I were threatened that if we told our mother, it would kill her and we'd all go into foster homes. We were routinely beaten and hid our bruises under long sleeved sweaters and shirts. I slept with a knife under my pillow.) There were secrets in my family: *Don't tell. Don't say a word.* Words were dangerous, powerful, could kill. Just the word *Yes* could kill my mother, my sisters and brothers. Could get me killed. Dead. What was that like? I could write and un-imagine it.

In my journal, I could write in rhyme. Make music. But quiet, so no one would hear my mistakes. In my journal words were kings and queens. They stayed still where I put them on their little lead-pencil thrones or I could move them around like chess pieces. Other girls had dollhouses. I had my journal, and I could make a dollhouse much finer than theirs with nothing but words. I could lift heavy furniture with the tip of a pencil. I could make brick chimneys, porches, windows, doors, secret passageways to cool basements. I could steal away.

Why did I do it? Why was writing in my journal so important to me? Some years ago, I discovered some of my old journals in a plastic bin in the carport. (No one would steal them except the rain). Many years later, I opened the bin and pulled out one of the ragged journals. There I was, a voice speaking to itself, a mind revealing itself to itself, a person coming into the world. I see now that I wrote to understand who I was, to become a witness to my life and to capture, without benefit of a camera, a certain slant of light. I saw that I had this habit of copying out passages of novels, poems, in my own hand, as if I had written them, could write them, as well as my own awkward attempts at poems. In those journals, I was practicing to become a writer.

Looking at a more recent journal I noticed a draft of a sonnet I tried to write about my husband who gives money to the homeless as we walk down the street. We are both poets, and so have little to spare, but he feels a sense of responsibility to these people. I'm less generous, more cynical and suspicious, and found myself really getting angry with him for "throwing money down the drain." He would quietly listen and even agree, but he wouldn't stop giving. Eventually, I found myself writing about my feelings in my journal, as a way to try to understand why there was this difference between us, who was "right" and who was "wrong." I knew if I wrote about it without strategy or form, I would simply be complaining and wasting a lot of ink. So, I gave myself the challenge to write "as if" I understood why he did it, with the compassion I lacked rather than with the anger I felt. Since I was reading Shakespeare's sonnets at the time, I decided to give myself the further challenge of writing in a loose sonnet form and rhyme scheme. This was my first draft:

> When he walks by the old drunk or the young
> vet, he rummages in his pockets for
> change or a stray bill, remembers the strong
> urge of fifteen years ago when his joy
> was trapped in a bottle, or in the tight roll
> of a joint passed from one set of dry lips
> to another. Their cracked palms open like scrolls
> toward the bright coins of light, chips
> of winter barter for the dark and narrow alleys
> of this city. And he doesn't much care
> what his money is exchanged for, a blanket,
> a pair of wrecked shoes, the harsh glare
> of a needle or a package of smokes.
> Each time he reaches toward them he's repaired;
> his own life changed again—altered, broken.
> Resurrected by gratitude. Spared.

I saw first that I couldn't stay to fourteen lines, and I couldn't get the rhymes to work, and I hated the ending that seemed too obvious and

wordy. I rewrote line after line trying to compress, to make the lines
cohere and still make sense. It seemed that the poem felt forced, no matter what I did. Finally, I discarded the tyranny of rhyme and wrote it in
free verse. My journal shows that I worked on the poem for months, trying to perfect it. I see now how I was also working on my heart, trying to
enlarge it. I had finally come to an understanding of my husband's need
to give in spite of my need to save.

What follows is the final version published in my third book, *Smoke:*

Figures

When he walks by an old drunk or a stumbling vet,
he stops to rummage in his pockets for change
or a stray bill, remembers the cold urge
of fifteen years ago that kept his joy trapped
in a bottle or in the stained nub of a roach
passed from one set of cracked lips to another.
Their creased palms open like scrolls
toward the bright coins of light, stamped chips
of winter barter for the scraps and opiates
of this city. He won't ask and doesn't care
what his money is exchanged for: a blanket,
a pair of wrecked shoes, the harsh, sharpened
glare of a needle or a pack of smokes.
Who can calculate the worth
of one man's pain? What they need, he figures,
can't be more than what he owes.

In my M.F.A. workshop I have my students keep a journal. The
M.F.A. program keeps them busy, perhaps along with working an extra
job on the side while caring for a family, eating, sleeping, keeping the bike
or the car in good repair, washing their hair. They thought being in a program would give them time to write. I tell them how it is in the program,
just like how it is after the program. There's never enough time to write.
So, we make time. I tell them to go home and think about what time is
the best for them for writing and what place. I tell them to experiment.
Go to a café, a laundromat, the train tracks, the park, a bus stop, or the
backyard. They come back. Some say they get their best ideas in the
shower. I tell them to put up a grease board in the shower. Some say they
get their best ideas while walking. They buy small notepads to carry in a

back pocket or purse. I tell them they must go to the place they've chosen and write for an hour each day. It's an assignment, part of their coursework. I tell them no one will read what they've written, not even me. They are to turn their journals in at the end of the term, but I'll simply skim the pages to see they've done the assignment. They're thrilled. They've been ordered to write.

Even when they get nothing to speak of, they're happy. They've written something. Even if it was only a list, a description, a thought they carried further than they might have had they not taken the time to explore it on paper, they're happy. Many get actual drafts of poems, and they begin bringing them into workshop.

"I wrote this on the bus."

"I wrote over the prescribed hour and was late for a conference, but I got this poem!"

They're ecstatic. It's working. Yes, I tell them, this is how you steal time from your life to write. When they are in full swing, I announce that the next assignment is to stop writing. I forbid them to write. Not one word. They are on the honor system not to write. They come in the following week, heads down, and guilt written all over their faces. They confess: they snuck, and wrote. I'm happy for them. I tell them to read us out loud something from their journals. On days like these, I feel less alone.

FORGETTING TO REMEMBER— WHY I KEEP A JOURNAL

Kyoko Mori

I

My grandfather, Takeo Nagai, was the first person I knew who was serious about writing. In the summers when my mother, brother, and I visited his house in the Japanese countryside, every afternoon Takeo sat down at his desk with his diary—a small notebook with a cover, a different color for every year—and composed his entries with a fountain pen. Every page, printed with the date on the right-hand side, had narrow black lines for him to fill with commentary. Like most old people, my grandfather wrote the traditional Japanese way, from top to bottom, right to left. He described the flowers blooming and the tomatoes ripening in the garden, the walks he took with my brother and me, the books he was reading and the neighbors who came to visit. Each day—no matter how eventful or quiet—was made to fit precisely in the allotted space. For my grandfather, writing was about discipline.

His desk was in the middle of his study, where we sat on the traditional *tatami* floor on thin cushions. Facing him across the desk, I worked on my "picture diary," a summer vacation assignment. In my notebook, the pages were divided in two: the top half was blank for pictures, and the bottom half was lined horizontally for writing. Because we were children, our words traveled sideways from right to left, Western-style. I described and illustrated my swim in the river, my brother and me eating watermelons in the garden and spitting the seeds on the ground, and Takeo showing us the summer constellations at night. I colored the swimmers with crayons and painted the river with blue watercolor. The oil in the crayons repelled the water and kept the figures from blurring. I wasn't a child who could stay within the lines. My pictures often crossed the divide and smeared the words. The long stories I told—complete with the things my mother, grandparents, or aunts had said—ran the bottom half and wound around the margins; the last few sentences were written sideways but going up, across the top, then down the edge of the paper. Takeo complimented my writing and drawing, but my notebook was a mess. I couldn't wait to be old enough to graduate from my childish pictures and keep a diary exclusively with words.

Takeo was an educated man who became a country schoolteacher and rice farmer after World War II, when the government took the land he was supposed to inherit from his parents and redistributed it among their tenant farmers. Instead of living on the rent he collected, he ended up teaching school by day and coming home to work the few rice paddies his family was allowed to keep. By the time I was in grade school, in the early 1960s, my grandparents were able to live modestly on his pension and on the money my mother and her siblings sent them from Kobe, Osaka, and Tokyo. Takeo finally had time to read and write, but he didn't resume writing poetry or start the book about Japanese literature he might have written if he had led a quiet life of a scholar. By then, he was in his sixties. The only people he knew, besides his family, were country schoolteachers and farmers.

My grandfather did not confide his regrets to his diary. The peaceful commentary he made about the weather, the garden, his reading, his grandchildren, and neighbors carried the burden of what he couldn't say even to himself. For him, keeping a diary—giving every day the same space and weight—was a discipline of containment. He was glad to see my diary with the words stretching beyond their boundaries because he knew how lucky I was to grow up in a different time.

My mother, Takako, escaped the poverty her family had been reduced to when she married my father—an engineer who was on his way to becoming a division head at a prosperous company in Kobe. Though my father, Hiroshi, was not faithful to her, it wasn't unusual for a man of his generation to have girlfriends or mistresses (called *Nigo-san*, or Mrs. Number Two). Takako thought she could accept the way her marriage had turned out, just as her father had resigned himself to becoming a farmer instead of a scholar. She told herself that she had my brother and me, a comfortable home, and a husband who provided well

Kyoko Mori

for her financially. Until I was ten, we lived in an apartment house near the sea, where her friends from the neighborhood gathered for needle-work and tea parties, which she had organized. Takako wrote weekly postcards to her parents about the flowers in her garden, the excursions she'd gone on with my brother and me, the clothes and the tapestries she was sewing and embroidering. The postcards were her versions of Takeo's diary—cheerful news that fit on one page in her neat handwriting.

When we moved to a new house in a quiet neighborhood up on a hill, Takako found herself spending the whole day alone while my brother and I were at school. Her friends couldn't easily visit since they lived an hour away, and the women in our new neighborhood were older, with retired husbands who were around all day and expected their wives to wait on them. Hiroshi seldom came home anymore. His two girlfriends called our house late at night, looking for him. Each cried when Takako or I answered and said he wasn't home because she knew then that he was with the other girlfriend. No longer able to overlook what a sham her marriage had become, Takako started confiding her thoughts to a diary.

Unlike Takeo's diary, Takako's didn't have dates printed on its pages. It was a small plain notebook with a red vinyl cover and horizontally ruled pages. The year was 1968; most adults wrote sideways by then. Takako marked the date of each entry, but she didn't write everyday. She started in January, wrote several pages once or twice a week until April, and then she stopped. All summer, she made only one short entry—like Takeo's— about her garden in July. Then she started up again in November when the weather turned cold and she felt trapped in a house she hated and in a marriage that no longer made sense. She wrote once or twice every week, always coming to the same conclusion: her life was a complete waste; even her children would be better off without her.

Takako left her diary on the kitchen table when she killed herself in March 1969. She had thrown out or burned the last few pages, leaving a crooked scissors-blade edge near the binding. I couldn't imagine what she could have written on those pages that were worse than those she'd left intact. When she first turned to her diary, she must have been hoping for a relief. She believed she could express her unhappiness, and once and for all be done with it, or maybe she was trying to put her feelings into words in order to contain them, the way her father had tamed his bitterness and regrets. However, her despair only got greater and greater the more she wrote about it.

I started keeping a diary when I was thirteen, the year after my mother's death. By then, my father had remarried, and I was no longer allowed to see my mother's family. No one at our house ever mentioned her. My brother, four years younger than I, called our stepmother Mother and followed her around the house, hanging on her every word. My father refused to give me Takako's diary, but I wasn't surprised anymore by anything he said or did. I wrote in mine because I was afraid of forgetting the life I once had with my mother.

My diary mixed the daily events—school, friends, books, sports—with the memories they brought back. I wrote about seeing my mother's favorite paintings again at the city museum I'd revisited with friends, walking in the public gardens she'd taken me to in Kyoto, and practicing the breast stroke she had once taught me in the river near her parents' home. At least in my notebook, the past and the present existed on the same page. I used the ruled composition books with speckled blue or black covers. At the time, I attended a bilingual junior high school. Because I suspected that in my absence, my stepmother looked through my desk drawers, I wrote in English—a language she could not read.

Perhaps it was this choice of language that, over the years, transformed my diary into a writer's journal: not simply a personal record of activities, reflections, and feelings, but a working notebook for words, images, stories, and ideas. A few years before I moved to the U. S.—first, to attend high school for a year at sixteen and then, at twenty, to finish the last two years of college—I was already learning that putting my daily life into words involved a kind of translation.

II

I write my journal entries by hand, with a blue Pilot Vball Extra Fine pen that has a see-through barrel—the ink inside sloshes up and down, making tiny bubbles. I've given up on fountain pens because they scratch, leak, and smear. The Vball pens write the way I imagine a fountain pen would—if I could only find the right one—smoothly with a light touch. An ideal notebook for a journal is a "blank book" with a pretty cover: marbled paper, art-deco designs, stenciled stars or flowers. A blank book is smaller than the speckled composition book and easier to carry around.

When I travel, I write in my journal everyday. In 1991, when I went back to Japan for the first time in thirteen years, my grandfather had been dead for ten years but my grandmother was still alive. I spent a weekend at the old house where she was living alone at ninety-three. We looked through the stacks of photographs she'd kept—some from before my birth—and she told me a story about each one. I went to bed in the same room where I used to sleep on our summer visits, woke up in the middle of the night, and walked into my grandfather's study. I sat at his desk, which was still in the middle of the room, and wrote down everything I could remember from my grandmother's stories about the photographs to the tiny red potatoes we dug in her garden. The rest of the trip, I saw my other relatives, my father and stepmother and a dozen old school friends. Because I was jet-lagged, I woke up at two or three every morning, ready to review the preceding day's events in my notebook. The moment my eyes opened was the only time I felt completely clearheaded. In one relative or friend's house after another, I sat in the empty kitchen with a glass of water, writing until dawn.

As soon as I returned to Green Bay, Wisconsin, where I was living at the time, the trip seemed more like a stray scene from my childhood than a recent event. The Japan of 1991 felt just as far away as my childhood, both in time and distance. This sense of distance was what I needed to write my memoir, *The Dream of Water,* but without my journal, I wouldn't have remembered enough details to reconstruct the scenes I put in the book. Though I had a handful of photographs I'd taken, I'm a terrible photographer—especially of landscape shots; I can seldom recall what I was trying to photograph because everything looks off kilter. During the trip, I'd jotted down reminders like "4 P.M. Meet Miya [friend] in Kobe" in my pocket calendar. The calendar helped me keep track of the sequence of events, but the brief notations wouldn't have made much sense without the journal, which described the green dress Miya was wearing when I spotted her at the train station, the iced coffee we drank at a café in the underground shopping center, and the eighth-grade skit we remembered together. Each time I opened the notebook, it was like stepping into the past—my recent trip and the more remote past of my childhood. This double sense of stepping back became essential to my conception of the memoir.

On my subsequent trips to Japan, or to Wisconsin where I don't live anymore, my journal has become more than a recording tool. I carry it around like an amulet as I bounce between nostalgia and fear—between the shocks of "How could I have left this place?" and "How could I have lived here at all?" I can see just how my life would have turned out if I'd stayed, and I'm amazed, once again, by how regretful and relieved I am about leaving. I want the visit to last forever, and I can't wait for it to be over. The journal allows me to immerse myself in this tremendous confusion without drowning. It reminds me that I'm here not only to experience everything but also to translate it into words. This very moment, too, will begin to make sense on its pages. Keeping a journal is the difference between living a life and writing about it.

When I'm home—which is now in Washington, D.C.—I don't write in my journal everyday. If I'm in the middle of a long writing project, months might pass between the entries. I can only come up with so many words every day, and I need to save the best for the book I'm drafting or the essay I've started. At these times, there's not much to record anyway, since, by design, I live a steady, uneventful life while working on a long project. When I take a break and turn to my notebook, it's to explore new ideas, images, or stories rather than to record anything specific. In fact, I need to write in my journal, because I don't know, anymore, what there is to record; I have to get to know my thoughts again. After a month or two of working on the same project, my mind feels both too full and too empty. There's nothing in my head, it seems, except the same old ideas I've been stuck on forever.

I start my journal writing by rereading the last entry to remind myself where I've been. Then I describe the few mildly interesting things I've seen or heard since that last entry, whether they come from my life or from my reading. I don't expect to be coherent or articulate. I let myself repeat or rephrase the same words and sentences as many times as necessary. I might begin with a list of furniture in someone's living room, the books on the coffee table, the colors of the dinner plates, salad plates, and coffee cups. Or maybe all the dinnerware was white and there were no books on the coffee table or anywhere in the house. I have no idea if any of this material will be useful in any way. Usually, the writing moves from description to speculation—"Why does so-and-so have furniture like this? Is this the kind of dinnerware I thought she would have? If not, what about this is surprising? What does it say about her, or about me for noticing it?"

The loose, speculative writing is a grownup version of the picture diary I kept as a child. I go over the same scene two or three times, using various methods that possibly conflict with each other and blur the picture, letting the words stretch beyond the lines and get messy. I allow my thoughts to roam and meander rather than come to any point of order too soon. In the process, I usually discover that my mind's not as empty as I feared. There are a lot of ideas I've been tossing around, and they even have an overall pattern or direction. A new realization has been shaping itself, trying to make itself known to me. I can almost articulate it. The journal, plus living alone, allows me to find out what my ideas are without boring another person with an observation I haven't yet made clear to myself, or worse, embellishing the words to entertain or impress the listener before I know what they really mean. In my notebook, I can look for the story I would tell if I wasn't playing to an audience.

My journal is a combination of my grandfather's and my mother's diaries. My thoughts grow bigger and repeat themselves like my mother's, though not with the same tragic consequences; and then they fall into order like Takeo's, although with much less discipline. I don't often reread the journal entries I've made when I wasn't trying to record a specific event. Those speculative entries are more like grocery lists and work without my having to read them. For example, half the time I drive to the Whole Foods store near my house, I get out of the car and realize I've left my list on the kitchen counter, but I don't rush home to get it. As I walk up and down the aisles inside the store, I can remember which items were on the forgotten list. Making the list has sorted out the groceries in the aisles inside my head. The right things resurface in my memory at the right time, because I've written them down. I keep a journal so I can forget everything and still remember it.

As important as my journal is to me, I wouldn't want the notebooks kept beyond my lifetime. Because I don't use my journal, usually, to rehash petty hurts and resentments among friends (they're not interesting enough to write about; they bore me even while they're happening), there isn't much in it that would hurt people close to me. The harsh observations in it are about people—like my stepmother and my brother—with whom I'm no longer in contact. I don't keep a lot of secrets in person or in writing. The details in my journal—about my marriage, for example— are earlier versions of the stories I ended up telling publicly, so there won't be big surprises for anyone. All the same, I don't want anyone reading my journal, in or after my lifetime, because the writing in it is not even remotely my best. The wordy, trite, repetitive sentences I scratched in my notebooks shouldn't outlive my need for them.

I'm going to leave my notebooks to my friend Jim, who is an artist and a Catholic priest. Jim takes the books from small-town churches and libraries that closed down and builds sculptures from them. The hardbound books, many of them with edges colored red, yellow, or green, are as cheerful as the blocks we played with as children. When he finds a particularly beautiful book no one wants to read anymore, he cuts out the middle and turns what is left into a shadow box, with beads and religious paintings placed inside like a reliquary. Or he crinkles all the pages till the book stays open like an accordion or a seedpod. I like to imagine the words falling off the edge to scatter and disappear.

KEEPING UP
WITH THE DAYS

Peter Selgin

There is no doubt in my mind that a demon has been living in me since birth. (David Berkowitz ["Son of Sam"] in his diary)

Apparently, I could be quite a showoff. Once, at a college dorm party, I engaged my fellow guests by dangling by one arm from the terrace railing. The dorm was in a high-rise building, the party on the fifteenth floor. Another time, in the parking lot of an abbey in northern Germany, a similar desperate bid for attention had me jumping backwards, or trying to, over a two-foot-tall post chain barrier. Apparently I was wearing cowboy boots; apparently the back of a heel caught; apparently I was out cold for two minutes. When I came to, I couldn't feel or move from the neck down. My first (apparent) words to my traveling companions: "Guys, I think I just ruined our summer vacation."

My nervous system recovered, but my memory didn't. I say "apparently," because I don't recall either scenario. Were it not for the testimonies of multiple eyewitnesses, I'd dismiss both stories as apocryphal. I wish, too, that I could blame my memory lapses on alcohol or mind-bending drugs. But I've never been much of a drinker, and drugs played no role in my behavior or my memory loss.

The reason I don't remember either incident is because I didn't write them down. For a period of about ten years, starting when I was a senior in high school, I was a compulsive diarist; you might even say an addicted one. Wherever I went, whatever I did, I carried a notebook with me and filled it with the flotsam and jetsam of my days. In the beginning these notebooks were oversized (twelve-by-sixteen inches, some even larger), of plain paper designed more for sketching than for scribbling, with spiral bindings that came untilled and caught on sweaters and in women's hair. In them I recorded things seen and done, snatches of conversations, lush descriptions of landscapes and rooms, of people I'd meet and places I'd visit. When at a loss for words I tossed in some sketches, too. But mostly I wrote. In fact that's just about all I did. For ten years I was a machine whose primary purpose was to turn life into words and feed them to my ravenous notebooks, like a mother bird feeding worms to her chicks.

To give you an idea of just how bad my habit was: dining among friends, I'd keep my notebook open next to my place setting, between salad bowl and bread-and-butter dish, and scribble away between bites of food and sips of coffee or wine. (The few notebooks I've kept from those addicted days all bear the ketchup, soy sauce, coffee, and wine stains.)

At first even my most indulgent friends balked at being shadowed by this recording angel, this stenographer escaped from the courtroom, this dime-store frère Goncourt. Those who didn't like it had a choice: they could grin and bear it, or they could stop being my friends.

I lost a lot of friends.

The ones I didn't lose got used to it, or they resigned themselves, I guess: I can't be sure. Honestly, their feelings weren't of that much concern to me. When it comes to an addict and his addictions, the feelings of others don't often count for much. And like all addicts I rationalized my behavior and its morality. After all, was not my habit as much a part of me as my arms and legs? Did my true friends—those capable of understanding me at all—not understand that to ask me to put my notebook away would have been like asking me to saw off my nose and slip it into my pocket? We were inseparable, my notebooks and I, like John and Yoko.

People think of diary keeping as a positive thing, a source of therapy and enlightenment, not to mention self-amusement. All over the country journaling workshops are the rage, with participants encouraged to unleash and unburden themselves daily in writing, to get to know themselves and tend their psychic and spiritual gardens. In the United States alone five million diaries or so-called blank books are sold every year (it wouldn't surprise me to learn that the number exceeds that of all annual first novel sales). In *Writing Down the Bones,* writing guru Natalie Goldberg instructs her disciples to "finish a notebook a month . . . Simply . . .

fill it. That is the practice." That is also a lot of notebooks. Julia Cameron's *The Artist's Way,* a twelve-step program for creative self-fulfillment that, among other things, encourages its adherents to journal every morning, has been an international bestseller for years. Diary keeping, a once utterly private and even—with its faintly imagistic undertones—distasteful act, has grown into a vastly popular pastime and a multimillion-dollar industry.

But is diary keeping good for you?

In my case, it wasn't. But then, I may have gone too far. I didn't just keep a diary; I kept it to an unhealthy extreme. My diary became not the place where I kept track of my existence, but where I lost it in a flurry of words, my spiritual garden choked with verbal weeds. My habit made me rude, terribly rude. I had no idea how rude I could be.

Well, I had some idea. One evening, on a double date in the East Village, I was given my comeuppance. My date was a Turkish conceptual artist named Gülsen (pronounced Goo-shen). We were gathered around her coffee table, drinking wine and eating caviar-stuffed eggs, when I got out my notebook and started writing. Gülsen, whose pencil drawings typically consisted of a single fine line drawn vertically down a sheet of tracing paper—a line so delicate you had to stand within centimeters to see it—and who could be as blunt in person as her drawings were subtle, put down her glass of wine and said, "Why don't you count the flowers in my vase, Peter, and write down the number? Or better still, why not take off all of your clothes, count your pubic hairs, and tell your notebook how many there are?"

I put the notebook away. But Gülsen's lesson was short-lived: You can't shame an addict into quitting. The next day I was at it again, and the day after that, scribbling away, trying in vain to keep up with the days.

For that was what my compulsion was based on: the notion that one could somehow hold on to one's life by putting it down in words, that in recording my experiences I was saving them, keeping them from being ground to smithereens in time's garbage dispos-all. With each tick of the clock another moment was gone, forgotten. My sense of loss was great, or would have been, but I had the cure: I would hoard and preserve my experiences, vacuum-pack them away like pears in Mason jars, trap them like flies in amber. I would rescue my past from oblivion.

Little did I know that by "rescuing" my life I would sacrifice it. Not only would I relinquish the past just like everyone else; I would lose my memories of those days; I'd trade them in for a tangle of useless, mildewy words.

My diary-keeping addiction didn't spring forth full grown and in armor like Athena from the forehead of Zeus. Its origins go far back. Though I wouldn't become a full-fledged addict until my twenties, I had my first taste of the wicked drug when I had just turned seven. For my birthday my mother gave me a diary: a four-by-five-inch book bound in synthetic white leather (which has since badly cracked), the words "EVERY DAY DIARY" stamped on the front cover over a cartoon basket of pink and red flowers. The pages inside were gilt-edged, ruled, and ticked off with the days of the month. At the top of each page the words "MY DIARY" in vehement all caps reinforced my already ironclad conviction that the little book had been manufactured for me alone.

The first entry is dated February 20, five days after my birthday. I quote it in full: "I went to the movie. The movie was all-western. I called it crap for babies."

You see here in embryo the critic I would become in my later years, as well as the full extent of my literary skills, which, over the next decade, would not improve considerably. I remember how possessively I clutched that little diary to my seven-year-old bosom, like a Bambuti tribeswoman suckling her newborn. I kept it in a carved wooden box behind my bed, locked away from my twin brother's probing fingers that I threatened to break if he ever touched it. Unlike everything else in our lives—our sweaters, our friends, the games that we played—this small book with its hideous floral cover was one thing I was not required to share, a sign that said, "I'm me—you're not!" With each word I entered into its gilt-edged pages, my sense of my own uniqueness increased.

But while part of me guarded my words, another, more hidden part longed to disperse them—like barbs from a porcupine's back. In addition to the days of the week, the diary had spaces set aside for "Special Events." Under one such heading I wrote:

"George Selgin stinks like the sewer he lives in. SUPER SECRET."

I see this as evidence that my "secret" diary wasn't so secret after all, that some part of me not only expected it to be read, but hoped, longed for it, as a hunter longs for the quarry to spring his trap. Come to think of it, isn't every diary a kind of booby trap to be sprung long after its keeper has set it and fled? A bomb with a very long fuse?

The entries in my EVERY DAY DIARY were sustained through Thanks-giving, when "we ate turky [*sic*] stuffing peas and an artichoke." Shortly afterward, my brother and I started a neighborhood club called U.N.C.L.E ("Unqualified Nazi Criminals Laundry Enamas [*sic*]"). Dues: 5¢. Objective: "But [*sic*] into peoples games and try to convince them your [*sic*] one of the players." Eight more entries follow, listing names of club members with dues paid or owed. Then the pages go blank and stay that way.

Six years passed before I kept my next notebook, this one assigned by my eighth-grade English teacher, Mr. Proudfoot, and referred to not as a diary but a journal—a prophylactic distinction designed to forestall visions of Ann Margaret scrawling in bathrobe and bunny slippers. It was the early 1970s, and mood rings, powder-blue leisure suits, and creative self-indulgence were all popular. Ira Progoff would soon start shucking his Intensive Journal Workshops. But Proudfoot was a step ahead of him. He had us write in our journals every day, spurred on by these words, sprawled in purple-blue ink e.e. cummings–style down an alcohol-scented mimeograph sheet:

> to be
> nobody but
> your-
> self
> in a world
> that
> keeps doing its
> best
> to make you
> somebody
> else

I took the words to heart. I tried as hard as I could to be nobody but myself. It wasn't easy, with everyone around me trying equally hard and using the same means. Still, it felt good getting up early every morning and writing in my journal over a mug of hot tea (not my father's bagged Lipton floor sweepings, but loose Formosa oolong, as Proudfoot and I had drunk it together, squatting at the Japanese-style table in the one-room apartment he rented at the edge of town). Scribbling in my journal made me feel mature, worldly—even a bit holy. I was thirteen years old.

Under Proudfoot's tutelage we did more than keep journals. We launched our school's first underground newspaper (knocked off on the same ditto master), wore love beads, and staged sit-ins against the Vietnam War. Two months before the school year's official end, Proudfoot left in a cloud of controversy.

With Proudfoot's departure again my notebook keeping entered a long hibernation, from which it didn't emerge until senior year, high school, with drawings—brazen caricatures of classmates and teachers—replacing words. These notebooks were practically community property, their pages greasy with the thumbprints of the curious, who passed them around as if they were oracles meant to be consulted in times of strife. Once, following my execution of a particularly brutal likeness of Madame Standish, my French teacher, I was sent to the principal's office. "Pete," Mr. Murillo said, shaking his bald head while examining my latest artistic affront, "how many times do I have to tell you to be more discreet?" Having pocketed my latest indiscretion for his growing collection, Mr. Murillo sent me on my way.

As senior year gave way to summer, and summer to backpacking in Europe, and Europe to art school in New York City, words crept back into my notebooks until—like kudzu strangling a forest—they took over again. Though I had no great command over them, something about words made them irresistible to me, possibly the fact that they weren't totally in my control. And so I wrestled with them, pinning them to page after page, not realizing that the words had me pinned, that my notebooks were writing me, displacing my life, consuming and ruining it.

Being an addict I saw none of this—or maybe I did see it, but I excused it, telling myself it was for a good cause, for Art with a capital *A*. I was an artist, burdened with an artist's dreams. One of those dreams was to produce a work unlike any other in its scale, rawness, honesty, and originality: a direct transcription of experience that would spare no one and hold nothing back. This work, which I titled "Pure Flux," would have no discernable plot, no theme, no consistent characters. It would be a work of chaos to match the chaos of life and would, in its own unique way, advance down that road well-trodden by Miller, Céline, Kerouac, and Alexander Trocchi (whose *Cain's Book,* a novel in journal entries about a heroin junkie living on a gravel scow in New York harbor, was the Holy Grail of my journal-keeping days), and a half-dozen other inveterate documentarians of their own dissolutions. Was I not preordained to produce a work to rival, if not surpass, theirs? Did I not have—as both a warning and a blessing—the words of Ralph Waldo Emerson, quoted in the epigraph of *Tropic of Cancer,* to guide and inspire me: "These novels will give way, by and by, to diaries or autobiographies—captivating books, if only a man knew how to choose among what he calls his experience that which is really his experience, and how to record truth truly."

If only! But I would know how to choose; I'd be one of those rare exceptions that prove the rule—the rule in this case being that life, whatever else it may be, is not a work of art. Bullshit! So I scribbled on, frantically, furiously, piling up notebooks like a bag person piling up magazines and newspapers, sure that all this piling on would add up to artistic triumph. Confronting me then with the distinction between literature and graphomania would have been as pointless as telling a bag person that his bundles of newspaper don't amount to shit, much less salvation.

Having started down this path, I couldn't stop; I had to keep going. Even if my notebooks all but choked me out of my real life, still, I believed in them. This is the diarist's dire fate, and why—taking Anaïs Nin to task for her own incurable habit—Henry Miller cautioned, "You will never keep up with the days. It will be like a big web which will strangle you."

Miller wasn't alone in condemning diaries. Immanuel Kant, among many others, warned his readers to avoid the practice, which, he said, paved the way to "lies, extravagance, distortion of perspective, perhaps even to madness itself." Ironically, some of the most convincing arguments against keeping a diary are made by diarists in their diaries. Of the futility of the enterprise the playwright Ionesco had this to say: "Literature is powerless. I can communicate this catastrophe to no one, not even to my wife. The unendurable thing dwells within us, shut in. Our dead remain in us. And why am I writing this journal? What am I hoping for? Whom can these pages interest? Is my unhappiness, my distress, communicable? Who would take on that burden? It would have no significance for anyone."

Ionesco joins hands with Sartre, who famously described all of literature as a form of neurosis. "Where there is no neurosis," said Sartre, "there is no literature, either." If all literature is neurotic, diary keeping is literature in its purest form. See the diarist locked up and scribbling away, generating enough morbid self-involvement to power a small eastern seaboard city. I scribble, therefore I am: such is the diarist's credo. No use explaining to him or her that a diary is to experience roughly what Cheez Whiz is to a cow. Or to put another way: Just because you muck the stable doesn't mean you know how to ride a horse.

But diarists aren't just neurotic, they're also liars and cheaters. Of her own diary keeping Anaïs Nin admitted "an incentive to make your life interesting, so that your diary will not be dull"—a statement that betrays her willingness to stack the deck of existence. When Oscar Wilde quips, "I never travel without my diary. One should always have something sensational to read on the train," he blurs the distinction between diary and novel. But that distinction will always be blurry, with diarists conflating transcription and embroidery. At the very least, a diary is selective experience. Intentionally or not, it lies through omission.

But then isn't the whole enterprise of diary keeping somewhat disingenuous, if not downright spurious? On the one hand, the diarist calls her pursuit intensely private; on the other, there is a record being made—for whom? Is there not, in the back of every diary keeper's mind, the desire—somewhere, someday, somehow—to be read? In *A Book of One's Own,* his deft survey of diarists and their diaries, Thomas Mallon writes, "Whether or not they admit it, I think all the purchasers of [diaries] have a 'you' in mind . . . Perhaps in the back of their minds, or hidden in the subconscious strata, but there." Mallon goes on to say, "In fact I don't believe one can write to oneself for many more words than get used in a note tacked to the refrigerator, saying, 'Buy Bread.'" A diary with no audience is like the proverbial tree that falls with no one there to hear it: that it exists at all no one can prove.

Now it seems that diary keepers are plagued with more than just the neurosis of their habit. A recent psychiatric study conducted in Great Britain shows that people who keep diaries are more likely to suffer from headaches, sleeplessness, digestive disorders, and "social awkwardness." The study upsets long-cherished views of diary keeping as therapeutic. In fact, among test subjects who'd undergone traumatic events, the diarists fared worst of all: they are more apt to "continually churn over their misfortunes," and as such are less likely ever to get over them.

So much for tending one's psychic garden.

By my twenty-eighth birthday I had filled over forty notebooks. But I didn't think of myself as a diarist, or of my notebooks as diaries. Nor did I view them, as many artists and writers see their notebooks, as the rough-and-tumble means to some perfected end, as scullery maids—rags on which to wipe their creative thoughts. As ever I looked to the exceptions, to works of art that began as notebooks and ended as masterpieces. No one would ever call Auden's *A Certain World,* Fitzgerald's *The Crack-Up,* or Cyril Connolly's *The Unquiet Grave* scullery maids. Yet these works more than qualify in style and content as notebooks.

But compared to what I had in mind, those were shapely, tidy volumes. My own notebooks would culminate in something far more grandiose and exhaustive, a work of gargantuan ambitions and proportions to shame *Remembrance of Things Past* or *Ulysses.* Pure Flux, the notebook of notebooks!

During those ten years I seldom kept one address for more than a few months. Not wanting to carry all those notebooks around, I'd ship them home to my mother, who stored them in the cellar of the house I grew up in on a Connecticut hill, and where a set of particleboard shelves groaned under their ever increasing weight. Whenever I'd visit home, I'd pull one down off the shelf, blow the furnace dust from its pages, sit on the guest bed, and read. Like Oscar Wilde before me, I found my own notebook entries highly amusing. There was the element of surprise, compounded with the joy of not recognizing oneself. To read those notebooks was to encounter this odd person who had been me, and whose thoughts in ways paralleled but did not entirely match my own. What a curious fellow, I'd think, flipping pages scented with mildew, reeking of a past all but forgotten, as if I'd never lived it. Over time, with repeated readings, the entries took on the quality of myths, replacing the past they were meant to preserve. Meanwhile my real past receded—like the lower layer of words in a palimpsest—growing fainter and fainter, until it disappeared entirely.

Not so long ago one friend reminded me of that episode in front of the abbey in Germany. More recently another friend told me of the time I dangled from that terrace. When I said I had no memory of these things, neither friend believed me. "How could you have forgotten?" Yet I had. Those episodes had escaped my notebooks; perhaps because they were so embarrassing, I had "neglected" to record them. Therefore they never happened; they didn't exist. Written words had crowded out genuine memories; diary had replaced memory. Where others had a cerebral cortex, medium temporal lobes, and a hippocampus, I had a bunch of fusty old notebooks.

I'm not sure what made me stop. Maybe it's because I began writing fiction, and publishing it. My dream of Pure Flux dissolved, replaced by more humble ambitions. After that, the few notebooks I kept were simply places to jot down titles and ideas, to work out a paragraph, to take down the name of a book recommended by a friend. Whenever the temptation to record my days crept up on me, I'd swat it away.

I'm not the only one to give up the habit. These days more and more would-be diarists have taken to the Internet. What would have been diaries a decade ago are blogs today. The supposedly private act of recording one's feelings has torn off its hypocritical mask and gone totally public, turning into a flagrant spectacle of self-indulgence at the computer keyboard. In the old days, writers drank in public and wrote in private. Now private vice and public performance have merged seamlessly. Booze gave us Hemingway, Fitzgerald, Joyce, Wolfe, Lowry, Faulkner . . . What will blogs give us?

A few years ago my father passed away. My mother sold the big house on the hill and moved to a condominium. She no longer had room for my notebooks. At the time my wife and I were renting a one-bedroom in Manhattan. We worked at home, with little room to spare. Still, for a while I kept the notebooks there: They were like a bunch of old friends who came to visit with no intention of leaving. The few times I'd take one down from the closet to dip into it, I started sneezing; I couldn't stop. Was it the dust and mildew or the words themselves that made me sneeze? Anyway, I was allergic to them.

One night I carried a notebook out to the compactor room, pulled the ovenlike door, took a deep breath, and, feeling as Abraham must have felt, braced myself. Then I let go. (I should have recycled, I know, but that would have meant putting it in the blue plastic recycling bin, from which I might have retrieved it.) As the notebook thumped its way down the chute, I waited to feel either horror or relief. I felt nothing. Not a thing. So I did it again. I threw a second notebook down the chute, and a third, a fourth, a fifth, a sixth . . .

It was past midnight. The rest of the building, including my wife, slept. I felt like a criminal. One by one the notebooks went down the chute, taking chunks of my ersatz past with them. In a sense, it was my youth going down that chute. I'd been holding on to it, thinking I might need it again someday.

With all but four notebooks gone, I crawled back in bed next to my sleeping wife and lay there, staring up at the dark ceiling, feeling not a sense of relief, exactly, but one of quiet accomplishment.

That was five years ago. I've not had one regret about throwing those notebooks away. They were the first very rough draft of a life that has since taken on some meaningful structure and shape and that has, if not a plot, at least a theme and some good characters. Like all rough drafts, it was a means to an end, something I had to go through to get where I am. And for that I'm glad.

But no, I don't miss a word of it. Why should I?

After all, I still have my memories.

ANNE FRANK REDUX

Karen de Balbian Verster

I began journaling around the age of thirteen after receiving a lined journal with lock and key for Christmas. Perhaps I took journaling as seriously as I did because I'd read *The Diary of Anne Frank* (begun when she was thirteen) and seen firsthand her hiding place in Amsterdam. Perhaps I was equally imprisoned by the loneliness and isolation that pervaded my life when my atheist father took a job in the Bible belt. Whatever the cause, I began journaling with a vengeance, and before the ink of my first entry dried my journal had become my best friend. To this day, it is my constant companion, there to share my appreciation for a bon mot, to help relieve a spell of boredom, to give solace when I've been ill treated, and to witness the profundity of my observations and ideas. (And it's all done so brilliantly! It's like watching myself bleed ever changing masterpieces.)

In 1979, I was in my early twenties, and being new to New York, I wrote about all the strange and wonderful things I saw there—the museum exhibits, modern-dance performances, black-box theatre plays, old movies. I wrote about what I was learning at Parsons School of Design, the students, the professors, and my projects. Here's an excerpt from my novel, *Boob: A Story of Sex, Cancer & Stupidity*, which I adapted from my journal:

> During my first year at Parsons School of Design, we all took school very seriously, as if our lives were at stake. This was reinforced by the professors who frequently regaled us with tales of "The Real World" we would encounter after we left Parsons. When we were given an assignment to alter our physical selves in such a way that our mental

selves were altered as well, I chose to be blind for twenty-four hours. I wrapped an Ace bandage around my head to prevent inadvertent cheating. I didn't worry what people thought of a person walking around looking like the Invisible Man, perhaps because it was for Art, but more probably because, being blind, I was oblivious to the stares I elicited.

I asked my best friend Nick, a gay guy who was more handsome and virile than any of the straight male students, to escort me to and from school.

"Sure, doll," he said.

Walking down Fifth Avenue, just before we got to the park, Nick said, "Hold on a minute. There's a hot guy I've got to meet." (Nick liked to scour the life drawing classes for well-hung male models and then drag me to the doorway to share his finds.)

I stood on the curb for the longest while. Nick wouldn't abandon me, would he? Finally, I lifted up the Ace bandage so that I could take a peek. There he was! Exchanging numbers with a guy on the next block. I sidled over to a building so I would be out of the way and then restored the Ace bandage to its blindfold function. Thank goodness my project was not ruined! I did a painting of a woman with no appendages who was swaddled in Ace bandages and being dragged along while sparks flew out of her brain, and got an "A."

I put myself through Parsons by bartending so bars became my home away from home. I wrote in bars because I wanted the company without the entanglements. My entries at that time are peppered with diatribes about how obtuse some guys could be when they chose to interrupt this vital endeavor—I mean couldn't they see I was *writing in my journal?* There I'd be, scribbling up a storm—(I've always been a steam-engine journal writer—full speed ahead—no pensive dabbling for me)—and they'd ask without fail, "Are you writing in your journal?" A bartender with whom I'd had a failed romance provided me with a witty comeback, "No, I'm just trying to see if this pen works."

In my early thirties, still writing in New York bars, I began to bewail the lack of men in my life. My excruciating analyses of why the latest man had dumped me were punctuated with Disney-esque descriptions of all the happy couples I observed canoodling around me, tweeting birds and all. Then I met my future husband and my journal became filled with the agony and the ecstasy of trying to get a man; and then, having married him, the agony and the ecstasy of trying to keep him. I started Freudian analysis around this time so I used my journal to record my nightly dreams and the interpretations my analyst and I arrived at. (How I miss my analyst—the only person in the world who listened to my chaotic, Technicolor dreams with bated breath.) Interestingly, all I have to do is to reread one of these descriptions, even from years ago, and it's as if I had the dream just the night before. I also made my first attempts at writing fiction, describing real scenes in my journal, which I thought might find a place in a future story. Here's another excerpt from *Boob: A Story of Sex, Cancer & Stupidity* that I culled from my journal:

The Museum of Modern Art was my home away from home. I purchased a membership so I could spend as much time there as I wished. After prowling though the museum, I loved to sit in the sculpture garden. I would sketch, read, write in my journal, ruminate, and watch people.

"Did you know this is the biggest pick-up spot in New York?" a man asked me.

I looked up from my book of Sherlock Holmes stories, not sure if I was interested. "Really?"

He sat down at my table. "Yeah. See that guy over there?" He pointed to a Rudolph Valentino type complete with long, white silk opera scarf.

"Yes."

"He's a regular. Here every week." He leaned towards me, and spoke confidentially. "He pretends he's the son of a Greek shipping magnate but he's really from the Bronx. And that guy over there— hold on a second. I'll be right back."

He jumped up and rushed away. I resumed reading my book.

The man returned, leading an attractive young woman by the hand.

"This is Juanita," he said to me. I was surprised that a woman with strawberry blonde hair and freckles would have a Mexican-sounding name.

"Hi. I'm Karen."

"Can you excuse me a minute?" the man said.

Juanita and I looked at each other while we tried to think of some conversational gambit. Juanita was the first to succeed. "How long have you known Barney?" she asked.

"That guy?" I said. "I just met him."

"Me too!"

"Well, Juanita, I think . . ."

"My name is Julia! He calls me Juanita because he said it fit my personality better."

Barney returned and we both turned to stare at him accusingly. "All right," he said, "I thought you were both attractive."

About ten years after graduating from Parsons, I took a creative writing class and was asked to write about the last time something happened. I chose to write about the last time I saw my dad who was dying of cancer. My journal supplied the backbone of the story since it contained specific, compelling details that I never would've remembered after the length of time that had elapsed—things such as the feel of a blueberry that has just been plucked, or how my dad's arms were made hairless from the chemotherapy. But mostly it contained descriptions of how my dad talked, which I used verbatim:

"God has forsaken me," my father said, exaggerating his voice like a member of the Peking Opera, an interesting technique that allowed him to be joking and serious at the same time. He made this statement while reclining in what he called his Frankenstein chair perhaps because he could crank it back—being a scientist, he liked to name things—in the study of his Angelica farmhouse.

"Maybe you have forsaken him," I tentatively replied. But my budding spiritual awareness was no match for Dad, who'd been a card-carrying atheist since before I was born.

"That's a crock of shit!" Dad loved a good argument. "First of all, there is no God. But if there were, it would be a She, because only a woman could fuck things up this badly."

Then, distracted by the sight of Calida placing a dish of scraps outside the kitchen door, he yelled, "Calida! If you'd stop feeding those kittens, they'd learn to hunt for themselves."

Apparently not hearing him—she knew how to win a debate with Dad—Calida let the door close without answering. Unwilling to abandon the thread of his argument, he turned to me. "Give a man a fish, and you've fed him for a day. But teach a man to fish and you've fed him for a lifetime. That's what I tried to do with Nerak, but she hasn't caught any fish yet."

When I was a child, Dad used to tell me stories about a little girl named Nerak who stupidly disobeyed her parents and got into terrible trouble as a consequence. It took me awhile to discover Nerak was my name backwards. If Dad hadn't revealed that the popping sound his nose made when he "adjusted it" was actually caused by him flicking his thumbnail against his front teeth, I'd still think he had a broken nose, too.

Now he peered at me from under his schnauzer eyebrows, his alert blue eyes the color of Delft china. He had a look I recognized, kind of stern and self-conscious at the same time, like he was willing me to appreciate his humor, his charm or whatever the hell one called this onslaught of personality.

I was thrilled when the final draft of this story, called "Teach a Man to Fish," was published in *Widener Review* in 1990. Then I got diagnosed with breast cancer, not once, but three times from 1991 to 1999. That's when journal writing saved my life. I wrote about all the things that no one could ever really understand, not my mother, my husband, not even someone who'd had the same diagnosis because the experience is as unique and impermanent as a snowflake. I wrote about my doctors, my research, my reactions, and other people's reactions. I wrote about all the crazy things I did to try to stay alive. I wrote about the death of my father-in-law from colon cancer in the middle of my chemotherapy. I wrote about the birth of my daughter after chemo had put me into premature menopause. I wrote about how I gave up hope after receiving my third diagnosis and about how I got my hope back after a year of despair. Cancer became a life-transforming event for me and I'm actually grateful I had it. I used a passage from my journal about getting radiation to begin the story "Tabula Rasa," which was published in *The Breast: An Anthology* in 1995 after having appeared in *Global City Review* in 1994:

> Every morning at nine o'clock I get my tits fried. Just one, actually. The right one. When I'm done I'm going to have a radiation barbecue. Cook the burgers right on my chest. This, the doctor says, is impossible because I'm not radioactive, but I like the image.

This opening line got the attention of *Publishers Weekly* when they reviewed *The Breast: An Anthology*:

> Even the writing on the most obvious topics (topless dancing, breast feeding) comes couched in moving and original presentations . . . Karen de Balbian Verster's fluid, moving story about a woman's [radiation treatments] begins "Every morning at nine o'clock I get my tits fried."

One story followed another and when I found I couldn't publish them as a collection, I determined to craft them into a novel. That's when I discovered the Achilles' heel of journal writing—I'd developed the deadly habit of telling rather than showing. After years of revising, I think I've finally learned to discern the difference and to consciously choose one over the other. The reward for all this hard work is that *Boob: A Story of Sex, Cancer & Stupidity* was published in 2005. Being the author of a published novel has rocketed me into another dimension of writing since it has made me feel confident enough to reveal the real me, the me of my journals. *You like me! You really like me!*

I'm now in my early fifties and I approach journal writing somewhat differently. I used to be a lot more compulsive about it: every entry had to be sequentially written until the journal was full. Each person had to be introduced and all the background information given before the tale could commence. I had a journal for each subject: a dream journal, a writing-idea journal, an experiential journal, a running journal, an art journal. My journals had to be beautifully bound, filled with 8 ½-by-11-inch unlined vellum. Now I use cheap composition books and affix art reproductions or photographs to their covers. The contents are a mishmash of subjects. I write big, I write small, on the lines or on an angle. I use several journals simultaneously and keep them in different locations—my purse, my desk, and my bedside table. They cover any topic that appeals to me at the moment, but I am scrupulous about dating them in order to preserve chronology.

I also don't write as voluminously in my journals as I used to. This is partly due to a less tempestuous life, and partly due to more professional writing opportunities. Every once in a while I'm in a situation where I'd die if I didn't have my journal so I can immediately process my emotions or any event that requires a 360-degree exploration. However, I generally use my journals more as workbooks or scrapbooks of ideas and information.

I still record my dreams. My dream descriptions will probably never make their way into my published writing because dreams are like your poop—no one is fascinated by them the way you are. Actually, I lie.

Here is an actual dream I used in my novel:

> After Dad died, Mom gave me the Kübler-Ross book [*On Death and Dying*], along with some birthday cards I'd made for him over the years. My therapist suggested that perhaps I got cancer as a way to be closer to my father.
>
> I dreamed I was watching a group of women on a hillside. They were using a piece of farm equipment, perhaps a combine. I realized they were mermaids. Suddenly, they all turned toward the sea as a large man rose from the water. In place of a penis was an octopus, tightly furled. "Let her go, let her go," they cried. He walked ashore and the mermaids got him by the legs and held him with the machinery. Slowly, the octopus unfurled its tentacles and the man removed a mermaid from its grasp. He let her go.

Now that I'm no longer in therapy, I like to describe my dreams in present tense and then I like to pick the strongest element of the dream and have a dialogue with it. I've learned a lot about my subconscious this way. I've also drawn images from my dreams. Rarely, I have a dream that provides the genesis for a story. Here is an actual dream I plan someday to develop into a novel or a screenplay which will be called "Thring."

February 28, 2006

The world has come to an end as we know it possibly due to the dearth of bees, possibly due to "Blindness," but it's chaotic. Hordes of people are fleeing the unnamed Canadian city where I'm attending a party with thirty to forty people when this occurs. We're eating hors d'oeuvres and discussing global warming. We stop to consider our options. I feel very strongly that we should get to BJs and stock up on food and batteries. I'm trying to figure out what food will be possible after the bees have stopped pollinating. The conversation drifts and I loudly resume my plea to get to BJs. Someone says, let's go tomorrow. I say, by tomorrow it will be too late. Then I realize it is already too late; BJs is most likely being ransacked as we speak.

The next morning we board a tour bus. We drive through streets teeming with people on the move. We do not know where we are going. We hope we'll know when we get there. I watch scenery through the bus window. It is mostly farmland dotted with buildings whose architecture appears to stem from a medieval Scandinavian period (if such a thing exists)—lots of gingerbread and onion domes.

We pull into a medieval Scandinavian truck stop for lunch. The restaurant is crowded but a sense of order prevails. We dine on cracker barrel choices.

We board the bus and resume our drive. As night begins to fall, we stop at a medieval Scandinavian industrial park and enter a large, abandoned building, some of whose windows have been broken. We appear to be the only people in the building. We make ourselves comfortable. I look out one of the broken windows at a landscape so moonlit it looks snowy. I wonder what the future holds.

In search of a bathroom, I encounter two people in a room. They are poking through all the machines and scientific equipment. One of them says, look at this, and holds up a video. Play it, I say, pointing to a VCR. We stand and watch as the video commences. It's in black and white with no gray areas. The images come and go faster than the speed of light. It is over before it has rightly begun. What was that I say, trying to make sense of the barrage of letters, designs and photos with which my brain was bombarded. But I am speaking to the empty air. The two people with whom I viewed the video are now fucking like rabbits on the littered floor. I watch for a moment, too surprised to be embarrassed. Then I sidle out of the room.

What happens next is that the video is a virus that lodges in the brain. One catches it through watching it, or interacting with someone who has. The virus causes loss of inhibition, and its aim is to consume as many healthy hosts as possible just for the hell of it—like computer viruses. At the end of this dream, I noted: Reread *The Hot Zone* and replicate viral behavior. Then combine with *The Ring, The Thing* with some *Aliens* ambiance thrown in.

Journal writing is like singing in the shower—I can let 'er rip without fear of judgment. And although it has given me some bad habits, it has also provided me with solace, entertainment, and enlightenment. Every time I go back and mine the raw ore of my subconscious I'm thankful I've pursued this endeavor. I will be a journal writer until the day I die, because as Anne Frank said, "I want to go on living after my death. And therefore I am grateful to God for giving me this gift . . . of expressing all that is in me."

JOURNALING WITHOUT
THE JOURNAL

Michelle Wildgen

My career in journaling began around age eleven and dissolved by my early twenties, but during that time I was a dedicated chronicler of my inner and outer lives. People gave me blank journals and I filled them and stacked them in a private desk drawer.

Now, in my early thirties, I have several unfilled journals in my desk. One is actually handmade, from its soft thick paper to the twine that keeps it closed to the cottony leaves of its cover. Its colors are muted and gentle; blossoms are pressed delicately between its layers. I can't stand to jot a thing onto its velvety surface.

The truth is that I have not used a journal in many years. Rather than jotting notes and thoughts in a handy book, I keep them in my head, and I hold off beginning a new project until I have a decent sense of where it's going. I can't really say this is the best approach for everyone, but when I have tried keeping a journal as a way into essays and fiction, the process invariably backfired. I wrote the notes, but when I looked at them again, an unpleasant alchemy had occurred. Recording these thoughts actually killed the impulse to turn them into story. I still believed in the idea of journaling but I was no longer successful at it myself. Clearly I had to find an alternative.

Those early journals of mine, a stack of bound books and ragged spiral notebooks chronicling adolescence through college, languished for years in a box in my mother's spare bedroom. Because their contents were hazy to me, I could be proud of them; their existence proved that I had been dedicated to writing even as a kid. Eventually my parents decided I should clear the notebooks out of their closet, because they needed the room or because the pong of adolescent self-regard had drifted into the hall. I quite gladly took the box and stuffed it into my own closet. At that time, I was in graduate school, writing away, and it seemed fitting that I should reclaim my early work.

Then came the day when I was working on a short story about a teenage girl. Finally, those old journals would come in handy! I dug them out, wiped the dust off their covers, and got reacquainted with my early self.

They were appalling documents. I don't mind all the racy things I did. I don't even mind so much the gullibility and solipsism, but I do mind the shitty writing. The snippets of fiction here and there, and my thoughts and ideas about writing, were the worst of all. Reading these journals was not only uninspiring; it was traumatic.

Here's a brief recap of my writings: Early on, I devoted pages to the usual discussions of family and friends. On the creative side, I scribbled novellas about grand romances and successful rock bands (all of my characters were sixth graders). An astute observer of pop culture would recognize a Madonna video ("Papa Don't Preach") as the source of inspiration for at least one story.

As I headed into my teens my topic remained the same: I was still writing grand romances and bad dialogue, but now it was nonfiction. I only had to transcribe it word for word from suburban Ohio teenage life. I glanced up from time to time and wrote about the world, I suppose, but for the most part the entries from that epoch focused on any display of interest from a high school boy, which would in turn spark my own far more intense interest in myself. If these journals had an omnibus title, that title would be "Here Are Some Things People Have Said to Me (About Me!)"

Once again, I stowed the journals away, needled by doubt whenever I let myself think of them. I thought what I was writing as an adult was worthwhile. But then again, I thought the same thing as a teenager. The evidence said otherwise.

Yet this is true of most of us, I imagine, and it's the rare writer whose early journals aren't embarrassing. The good part about that period is I was already attempting to be a writer. I wrote each day, sometimes a paragraph and sometimes ten pages, and I thought I would always do so. But my particular love of journaling—not everyone's, by any means, but mine—turned out to be like my love of the American rock group The Doors. It had a lot more to do with youth than I'd realized. When I grew out of delineating each romantic turn, when I fell in love and stayed there and was no longer alert to every nuance of every new guy I met and every possible perception of me, I stopped writing in journals. Twenty-one years old and I was already sick of myself. I had always used a journal for the furtherance of total narcissism rather than craft, and I have never been able to shake the association when I sit down to try journaling as an adult and as a professional would—a blend of personal and literary thought, as a response to books, art, and movies, and as a record of the thoughts and images that could spark the next round of work.

When people ask if they should journal, I still say yes, absolutely, and I really mean it. And I've kept trying to do so myself. I've stayed alert to ideas and jotted them down and none of them became stories. The notes left me as nonplussed, even embarrassed, as I had been by my teenage journals. "Cat—moon—open door?" What was I going to do with that?

I came to realize that for me it is a question of *when* I write down an idea. If I try to use a journal to catch it at the first appearance, if I try to give it words without finding the fictional context first, its magic departs. For me, committing an idea to words too soon can flatten out the whole thought, from a world to a postage stamp. It's no longer the glowing thing I've been circling in my head, enjoying its presence, refusing to scare it away until I really think I'm ready to try and work with it.

So how do I get anything done? The answer is that I can and do walk around with an idea in my head for weeks, seeing its silhouette behind a screen in the corner of my eye, aware of the tactile pleasure of its weight and curves. My brain can cradle an unformed idea like a ripe peach in the hand, and it has to, because it's the only thing that works for me. You could say I'm journaling in my head, following the same creative paths without writing it down. This method works particularly well when the mind is only lightly occupied—three-mile walks in the mornings, a long quiet drive, or cooking a dish I've made a hundred times before. I've learned to let the mind amble where it likes, and it does the work. Say that for some time I have had a particular image in my head, or a phrase, something small and incomplete: a faith healer, with his vial of oil in a little bag; a house in the center of a field. I will then wander around for a few weeks trying to explore, in the back of my head, where the faith healer came from, where he's headed, and who will be anointed with that oil. I have to do this in very concrete ways—I don't mean the grand arc of where that faith healer is headed as a human being. I mean, "The faith healer is in his car, driving. Where will he be when he gets out of the driver's seat?"

Or I may not have a character in the image—it may be an object, or a sensation phrased in a very particular way. Then I turn it over for some time, trying to define what emotions that image evokes, and where the emotion leads. The image itself—crab apple trees in bloom very early in the morning, the corn in an empty field shifting as wild turkeys move through it—may end up so embedded in the story that to the reader it won't be recognizable as the source of the fiction. To the reader it may finally be simply a part of the whole, a nice phrase paused over and then moved past. I don't regard this as a problem, though there is something bittersweet about letting your lovely phrasing take a back seat to a larger story, like watching an adorable child grow into someone older, someone different, but someone more complete. That's how this kind of mental play goes—solutions present themselves, characters thicken into existence, the plot stretches out a slim new tendril, and you follow it. And then it's time to return to the computer.

I believe in being aware of your own writing rhythms and habits, taking note of what helps and what doesn't. I write for a few hours in the mornings, on the weekends, but not at night. I know when to put down the detective novels that relax me and turn to the literature that inspires me. I've learned when to bake bread or take a walk—and forego the iPod if I'm really serious—and I've learned to be alert to the moment when I can stop journaling in my head and sit down to write.

APPENDIX I

Use Journaling to Spark Your Writing

Diana M. Raab

When my mother gave me my first journal when I was ten, I had no idea that this seemingly benign gesture would lead to a lifelong passion for writing. The blank notebook had quotations from the mystic poet and painter Kahlil Gibran imprinted on the top of each page, designed as inspirational sparks for the budding writer.

The journal was a gift to help me cope with the tragic death of my grandmother, who until that time had been my caretaker. My mother knew that journaling had helped my grandmother navigate through difficult times and so she thought it could be useful for me, too. That early gift and the subsequent days I spent writing in my walk-in closet helped shape my love for journaling, a passion I've carried into adulthood.

While studying creative nonfiction during graduate school, I stumbled upon the diaries of writer Anaïs Nin, who also began journaling at a time of loss—about the time her father left the family for another woman. Nin was only twelve, and her first journal entry was a letter to her estranged father. After filling the pages of my own journals and reading Nin's, I discovered the value of the journal as both a literary work in and of itself, and as a seeding ground for future works.

Today, in the writing classes I teach, I stress the importance of journal keeping as a powerful tool for creative expression and self-healing, and a way to help solidify thoughts in both one's personal and literary life. A journal can be a veritable treasure chest of thoughts and anecdotes. It is not only a place to collect ideas, though, but a place to practice writing and overcome writer's block.

My first book, *Getting Pregnant and Staying Pregnant: Overcoming Infertility and High-Risk Pregnancy,* began as a journal chronicling my eight months of bed rest while carrying my first daughter. Back in the 1980s, I didn't think anyone would be interested in reading a day-by-day account of my experience, despite the insights I could provide, yet, coupled with practical information gleaned from my nursing background, a self-help book evolved. Here's one of my journal excerpts that later became part of the book's introduction:

> Finally, at thirty-two weeks, approximately four weeks short of what is known as the term of pregnancy, I gave birth by cesarean to a beautiful 4 ½-pound girl. Although she didn't cry at birth and was completely blue, it was the happiest moment of my life. Her first few moments of oxygen support were enough to give her the strength to carry on a life of her own.

In my recent memoir, *Regina's Closet: Finding My Grandmother's Secret Journal,* I used journal entries I had written years earlier as I was coming to grips with the loss of my grandmother. Writing about this painful event was cathartic, and the journal entries became the foundation for the memoir's first few chapters. In the book's final draft, I included one of the passages from my journal where I discuss my grandmother's death scene: "Soon I spotted two paramedics grasping both ends of the stretcher my grandmother was strapped to. With quick and urgent steps, they transported her down the steep stairs leading to the front door. I wondered what would happen if they slipped and Grandma went flying." In addition to books, my own journaling has led to a number of published articles, including "Lucknow Woman," an award-winning essay pulled from a part of my journal where I wrote volumes about coping with breast cancer.

As a writer, you ought to keep—and carry—a notebook for several reasons, says fiction writer John Dufresne. "A notebook is a reminder that you're a writer and that what you're currently doing while you're out of the house, away from the desk, is taking notes toward your next novel [or book]. You know that you think differently when you have a pen in your hand. You think differently and you observe differently. You see what's really there, not what's supposed to be there. You keep a notebook to teach yourself to pay attention. You keep a notebook to encourage yourself to crest. You keep a notebook to serve notice to the world—Writer at Work!" (Dufresne's comments and those of other writers in this article were sent to me as part of a book I am editing about journaling.)

I suggest the following tips to all writers, either beginning or advanced:

Start with the Proper Tools

This includes a good notebook and pen. Choose a notebook or journal that inspires you to crack it open. It should have a cover that appeals to you and feels good in your hands. It should lie flat so you're not battling with the binding. Some writers carry a smaller journal in their purse or pocket and a larger one in their office or car. "The notebook should be small," says poet Kim Stafford, whose latest collection is *A Thousand Friends of Rain*: "Shirt-pocket size. The size of the palm." In this regard, he goes on to say, "One definition of poetry: Any utterance that sings in short space."

Kyoko Mori, a poet, novelist, and nonfiction writer, believes the ideal journal notebook is "a 'blank book' with a pretty cover: marbled paper, art deco designs, stenciled stars or flowers." A blank book, she says, "is smaller than the speckled composition book and easier to carry around."

These days, some writers are taking to the computer for journaling. "The pocket notebook is for the hint, the computer for the deluge," Stafford observes. "The notebook is for the first move in what may be an interlocking sequence of poetic lines—a fragment with rhythm, voice, and atmosphere whispering in my ear. The computer is for the encyclopedic mass of resonant data impinging deliciously on the mind."

Experiment to see which type of journal works best for you. Your choice may also depend upon your mood. One day you might prefer a leather-bound lined journal, while another day a woven exterior with an unlined, recycled interior may feel right.

Your pen should be comfortable in your hand and the ink should flow smoothly. Most writers are quite particular about their pens. I prefer gel pens, and for some reason, my creative juices flow best with purple ink. Experiment with different types of pens. "I use a blue Pilot Vball Extra Fine pen that has a see-through barrel—the ink inside sloshes up and down, making tiny bubbles," Mori says. "I've given up on fountain pens because they scratch, leak and smear."

Make Journaling a Habit

Try to write at the same time each day and be sure to date your entries. Choose a time when you're at peace with yourself, whether it's first thing in the morning or at night before retiring. Anaïs Nin wrote in her diary at night. Virginia Woolf liked to write following her afternoon tea. Some writers enjoy burning a candle while journaling—for them it inspires and sparks a creative mood. I suggest you find "a room of your own," à la Woolf, whether real or imaginary. It should be a place where you want to go, preferably not your desk, which can be too distracting. A good choice might be an easy chair or a coffee shop. It should be a place that relaxes you while sparking your creativity. Keep your journal in a spot where you'll see it every day and can't avoid it.

Put the Inner Editor and Critic Aside and Let Down Your Guard

In the world of journaling, spelling, grammar, and neatness do not matter. Fight the impulse to edit. Try not to erase or tear out any pages of your journal, even if an entry seems silly or trivial. You never know when the information might be useful later.

Allow your guts to spill out. Write openly. Brag, exaggerate, be happy or sad, and be honest. The journal is a place where you can shed the mask you wear during the course of your day. You'll see that in time, your natural, authentic voice will emerge on the pages of your journal—a voice free from societal restrictions and inhibitions.

Allow your thoughts to fall from your subconscious. "I've used my journal more self-consciously, as a kind of writer's sketchbook, a place to try out ideas," says Robin Hemley, director of the nonfiction-writing program at the University of Iowa. "So besides overheard dialogue, I have included in my journals plot outlines, story ideas, character sketches, anecdotes that have been told to me, dreams, images, diarylike episodes —the occasional grocery list."

Some writers, including me, write first drafts of essays, stories, or poems in their journals. For me, it's the only way to get completely in touch with my words and feelings. It's good to have a record of one's initial inclinations, thoughts, and inspirations, regardless of whether they end up in finished works. Anaïs Nin used long passages of her diary in her fiction. In volume four of her journals, she discusses how the two merged at a time when she came to an impasse in her fiction writing. You may find that you do some of your best writing in your journal.

Write Letters in Your Journal

Write to your characters, friends, loved ones—dead or alive. A mother may write a letter to her unborn child. A son might write a letter to his mother. A woman may write a letter to a friend to try to solve a disagreement. Letters allow a deep expression of emotions. You might write something in a letter that you can't express verbally. You may even decide to send the letter, but if you don't, that's okay, too. "People frequently write letters in their journal to those who have emotional significance in their lives," Tristine Rainer says in her book *The New Diary.* "Just as a diary doesn't have to be a record of activities, a letter doesn't have to be a report of the weather and the news since you last wrote. It can be an exploration of whatever a particular person evokes when you think of them."

Organize Your Journal

This task is of particular use to writers, to facilitate future access. There are a number of ways to organize your journal. I usually divide mine into three main sections. The first is designated for random thoughts, observations, snippets of conversations, comments. The second is dedicated to quotations that inspire me. The third section is for my poems, either in their entirety or in the raw form of images, phrases, and lines. I reserve the last few pages of the journal for a running list of books I'd like to read.

If you don't want to be bothered with sections, try color-coding, with pens or a highlighter, after the journal is completed. For example, you can use purple for reflections, green for quotations, red for possible story ideas, and yellow for notes from workshops or conferences.

You may also decide to keep individual subject journals to make re-reading easier. Some types of journals include:

A **personal-growth journal**, where the writer works out difficult situations.

A **crisis journal**, in which a crisis is used as a catalyst for writing. Use it during tumultuous times, or when life takes an unexpected turn or is in flux, and it can help anchor you.

A **therapeutic journal**, which is similar to a crisis journal except that it tends to be in diary format, chronicling day-to-day events.

A **gratitude journal**, which is a place to record what you are thankful for in life. This type of journal nurtures a positive outlook and is a good thing to have when you're feeling down.

A **smile journal**, which consists of things and events that make you laugh. (Keep in mind that humor heals.)

A **travel journal**, which is a place to chronicle journeys and trips, and include impressions and reflections.

A **dream journal**, which is typically kept at the bedside and written in first thing in the morning, even before a writer gets out of bed, as a way to tap into the subconscious mind.

A **transition or transformation journal**, which is used during transitional periods such as divorce or relocation.

Reread and Use Journal Entries for Future Works

After a time lapse, it's interesting to go back and reread your journal entries. You'll encounter memories, facts, questions, and reflections that might serve as a spark for a new writing project. You'll also detect patterns in your writing style and subject matter, and may be surprised by obsessions you repeatedly write about.

How you use your entries in writing depends on your genre. Many poets, it seems, carry journals to jot down snippets of images and phrases. Poet Denise Duhamel told me she sometimes lifts entire prose poems from her journals, in the same way poet James Wright was known to do.

Mori used her travel journal entries from Japan to write her well-received memoir *The Dream of Water,* in which she attempts to come to terms in her native land with the memory of her mother's suicide and the family she left behind thirteen years before. "Without my journal," she confesses, "I wouldn't have remembered enough details to reconstruct the scenes I put in the book. . . . During the trip, I'd jotted down reminders like '4 P.M. Meet Miya [friend] in Kobe,' in my pocket calendar. The calendar helped me keep track of the sequence of events, but the brief notations wouldn't have made much sense without the journal, which described the green dress Miya was wearing when I spotted her at the train station, the iced coffee we drank at the café in the underground shopping center, the eighth-grade skit we remembered together.

Every time I opened the notebook, it was like stepping into the recent past of my trip and the further back past of my childhood. This double stepping back became essential to my conception of the memoir."

Many poets keep journals because it's an ideal place to jot images or thoughts that might later turn into a poem. Poet Mark Pawlak says his notebook, "besides being a connection to my interior self and a way of perceiving the world, was a place for me to work out my ideas about poetry, and a place to chart the evolution of my own work and where it was heading." Some poets, Pawlak and myself included, use the journal to flesh out their own poetics by jotting down lines, poems, or complete thoughts of other writers and poets. Pawlak, for example, found himself inspired by Thoreau's journals and was inspired to mine the material from his own notebooks and organize it after Thoreau's example. "This approach led me to write several essays on poetry, on editing, on class, and on ethnicity," he says.

Read the Journals of Published Writers

This is not only a way to get inside their heads, but a chance for us to hear their raw and unedited voices. A journal is the voice of our true emotions and often includes stream-of-consciousness writing that speaks directly from the heart. Besides devouring Anaïs Nin's journals in graduate school, I read the journals of other well-known writers, including John Cheever, Gustave Flaubert, May Sarton, and Virginia Woolf.

There are as many ways to journal and use journal entries as there are ways to write. The important thing to remember is that there is no wrong way to journal. You are writing for yourself. Have fun and remember: What you write is for your eyes only. This might be the only writing genre where you won't receive one rejection slip!

APPENDIX II

A Journaling Workout

Diana M. Raab

Write a letter to someone, dead or alive.
Write about a transforming moment in your life.
Write about a trip you took that left a huge impact on you.
Write about a loved one, colleague, or mentor who has been influential in your literary life.
Write about what worries you.
Write about an accomplishment.
List some memorable moments in your life. Choose one to write about.
Write about a special occasion when everything didn't go as planned.
Write about your happiest and saddest moments.
Recount a personal experience that led to personal growth.
Write about something you've collected.
Write a sentence beginning with "I remember."
Describe a smell that brings back fond or unpleasant memories.
Describe a moment of utter depression when you felt so low you didn't know what to do.
Describe a significant quarrel between you and a family member.
Describe losing someone you really loved.
Write about a strange family member.
Write about what you remember about sixth grade.
Write about a memory with a bicycle.
Write ten ways you felt different as a child.
Write about what you are grateful for.
Write about the song that had the most impact on you.

Write about your favorite book.

Write about one of your grandparents.

Write about something you want but cannot have.

Free-write or write for fifteen to twenty minutes without lifting your pen off the page; ignore your inner critic; write about anything that pops into your head.

SOURCES AND
FURTHER READINGS

Published Journals and References

Alcott, Louisa May. *The Journals of Louisa May Alcott.* Athens: University of Georgia Press, 1997.

Apte, Helen Jacobus. *Heart of a Wife: The Diary of a Southern Jewish Woman.* Edited by Marcus D. Rosenbaum. Wilmington, Del.: Scholarly Resources, 1998.

Bashô, Matsuo. *The Narrow Road to the Deep North and Other Travel Sketches.* Translated by Nobujuki Yuasa. New York: Penguin Books, 1967.

Bass, Rick. *Oil Notes.* Dallas: Southern Methodist University Press, 1995.

Bond, Ruskin. *Landour Days: A Writer's Journal.* New York: Penguin Group, 2004.

Bukowski, Charles. *Notes of a Dirty Old Man.* San Francisco: City Lights Books, 1981.

Camus, Albert. *Notebooks 1951–1959.* Vol. 3. Translated by Ryan Bloom. Chicago: Ivan R. Dee, 2008.

Cheever, John. *The Journals of John Cheever.* New York: Knopf, 1991.

Chopin, Kate. *Kate Chopin's Private Papers.* Edited by Cheyenne Bonnell, Marilyn Bonnell, Per Seyersted, and Emily Toth. Bloomington: Indiana University Press, 1998.

Emerson, Ralph Waldo. *Emerson in His Journals.* Edited by Joel Porte. Cambridge: Harvard University Press, 1982.

Engel, Richard. *War Journal: My Five Years in Iraq.* New York: Simon & Schuster, 2008.

Filipovik, Zlata. *Zlata's Diary: A Child's Life in Wartime Sarajevo.* Translated by Christina Pribichevich-Zoric. New York: Penguin Group, 2006.

Fowles, John. *The Journals, Volume 1: 1949–1965.* Edited by Charles Drazin. New York: Knopf, 2005.

———. *The Journals, Volume 2: 1966–1990.* Edited by Charles Drazin. New York: Knopf, 2006.

Frank, Anne. *The Diary of a Young Girl.* New York: Bantam Books, 1947.

Friedman, Saul S., ed. *The Terezin Diary of Gonda Redlich.* Translated by Laurence Kulter. Lexington: University of Kentucky Press, 1999.

Gammel, Irene, ed. *The Intimate Life of L. M. Montgomery.* Toronto: University of Toronto Press, 2005.

Gaugin, Paul. *Noa Noa: The Tahiti Journal of Paul Gaugin*. San Francisco: Chronicle Books, 2005.

Gide, André. *Journals*. Vol 2., *1914–1927*, edited by John Miler and Justin O'Brien. Chicago: University of Illinois Press, 2000.

Gilman, Charlotte Perkins. *The Yellow Wallpaper and Other Writings*. New York: Bantam Books, 1989.

Grimké, Charlotte L. *The Journals of Charlotte Forten Grimke*. Edited by Brenda Stevenson. New York: Oxford University Press, 1988.

Klee, Paul. *The Diaries of Paul Klee*. Edited by Felix Klee. Berkeley: University of California Press, 1964.

Koppel, Lily. *The Red Leather Diary: Reclaiming a Life through the Pages of a Lost Journal*. New York: HarperCollins, 2008.

Lamott, Anne. *Operating Instructions: A Journal of My Son's First Year*. New York: Knopf, 2005.

Lerman, Leo. *The Grand Surprise: The Journals of Leo Lerman*. Edited by Stephan Pascal. New York: Knopf, 2007.

Lindbergh, Reeve. *No More Words: A Journal of My Mother, Anne Morrow Lindbergh*. New York: Simon & Schuster, 2001.

Merton, Thomas. *The Intimate Merton: His Life from His Journals*. New York: HarperCollins, 2001.

Nin, Anaïs. *Diary of Anaïs Nin*. Vols 1–4. Edited by Gunther Stuhlmann. New York: Harcourt Brace, 2003.

———. *Fire: From "A Journal of Love": The Unexpurgated Diary of Anaïs Nin, 1934–1937*. New York: Harcourt Brace, 1995.

———. *Henry and June: From "A Journal of Love": The Unexpurgated Diary of Anaïs Nin, 1931–1932*. New York: Harcourt Brace, 1990.

———. *Incest: From "A Journal of Love": The Unexpurgated Diary of Anaïs Nin, 1932–1934*. New York: Harcourt Brace, 1992.

———. *Linotte: The Early Diary of Anaïs Nin, 1914–1920*. Vol. 1. New York: Harcourt Brace, 1978.

———. *Nearer the Moon: From "A Journal of Love": The Unexpurgated Diary of Anaïs Nin (1937–1939)*. New York: Harcourt, Brace, 1996.

Nin, Anaïs, with Henry Miller. *A Literate Passion: Letters of Anaïs Nin & Henry Miller, 1932–1953*. New York: Harcourt Brace, 1987.

Oates, Joyce Carol. *The Journal of Joyce Carol Oates: 1973–1982*. Edited by Greg Johnson. New York: HarperCollins, 2007.

Plath, Sylvia. *The Unabridged Journals of Sylvia Plath*. Edited by Karen V. Kukil. New York: Knopf, 2000.

Rand, Ayn. *The Journals of Ayn Rand*. Edited by David Harriman. New York: Plume, 1999.

Sand, George. *The Intimate Journal*. Edited and translated by Marie Jenney Howe. Chicago: Academy Chicago Publishers, 1998.

Saroyan, William. *Days of Life and Other Escapes to the Moon*. New York: Dial Press, 1970.

Sarton, May. *At Seventy: A Journal*. New York: W.W. Norton, 1993.

————. *The House by the Sea.* New York: W.W. Norton, 1995.

————. *Journal of a Solitude.* New York: W.W. Norton, 1992.

————. *Recovering: A Journal.* New York: W.W. Norton, 1997.

Seferis, George. *A Levant Journal.* Translated by George Roderick. Jerusalem: Ibis Editions, 2007.

Shonagon, Sei. *The Pillow Book.* Translated by Meredith McKinney. New York: Penguin, 2007.

Thoreau, Henry David. *The Heart of Thoreau's Journal.* Edited by Odell Shepard. Mineola: Dover Publications, 1961.

————. *The Journals of Henry David Thoreau: 1837–1861.* Edited by Damion Searls. New York: NYRB Classics, 2009.

Woolf, Virginia. *A Writer's Diary.* Edited by Leonard Woolf. Boston: Mariner Books, 2003.

Books on Writing

Atwood, Margaret. *Negotiating with the Dead: A Writer on Writing.* New York: Cambridge University Press, 2002.

Berg, Elizabeth. *Escaping into the Open: The Art of Writing True.* New York: Harper-Collins, 2000.

Bradbury, Ray. *Zen in the Art of Writing: Releasing the Creative Genius within You.* New York: Bantam Books, 1995.

Cameron, Julia. *The Artist's Way.* New York: Penguin Group, 2002.

DeSalva, Louise. *Writing as a Way of Healing.* San Francisco: HarperSanFrancisco, 1999.

Dillard, Annie. *The Writing Life.* New York: Harper Perennial, 1990.

Eiben, Therese, and Mary Gannon; eds. *The Practical Writer: From Inspiration to Publication.* New York: Penguin Group, 2004.

Flaherty, Alice W. *The Midnight Disease: The Drive to Write, Writer's Block and the Creative Brain.* Boston: Houghton Mifflin, 2004.

Frank, Thaisa, and Dorothy Wall. *Finding Your Writer's Voice: A Guide to Creative Fiction.* New York: St. Martin's Griffin, 1996.

Goldberg, Natalie. *Thunder and Lightening: Cracking Open the Writer's Craft.* New York: Bantam Books, 2000.

————. *Wild Mind: Living the Writer's Life.* New York: Bantam Books, 1990.

————. *Writing Down the Bones: Freeing the Writer Within.* Boston: Shambhala Publishing, 2005.

Johnson, Alexandra. *The Hidden Writer: Diaries and the Creative Life.* New York: Anchor Books, 1997.

————. *Leaving a Trace: On Keeping a Journal.* New York: Little, Brown, 2002.

Klauser, Henriette Anne. *With Pen in Hand: The Healing Power of Writing.* Cambridge: Perseus Publishing, 2002.

Kramer, Mark, and Wendy Call, eds. *Telling True Stories.* New York: Plume Books, 2007.

Lamott, Anne. *Bird by Bird: Some Instructions on Writing and Life.* New York: Doubleday, 1994.

Lopate, Phillip, ed. *The Art of the Personal Essay: An Anthology from the Classical Era to the Present.* New York: Anchor Books, 1995.

McClanahan, Rebecca. *Word Painting: A Guide to Writing More Descriptively.* Ohio: Writer's Digest, 2000.

Moore, Dinty W. *The Truth of the Matter: The Art and Craft in Creative Nonfiction.* New York: Longman, 2007.

Pennebaker, James W. *Opening Up: The Healing Power of Expressing Emotions.* New York: Guilford Press, 1997.

Rainer, Tristine. *The New Diary.* New York: Jeremy P. Tarcher, 2004.

Root, Robert L, Jr., and Michael Steinberg, eds. *The Fourth Genre: Contemporary Writers of / on Creative Nonfiction.* New York: Longman, 2009.

Sher, Gail. *One Continuous Mistake: Four Noble Truths for Writers.* New York: Penguin Group, 1999.

Stafford, Kim. *The Muses among Us: Eloquent Listening and Other Pleasures of the Writer's Craft.* Athens: University of Georgia Press, 2003.

Tiberghien, Susan M. *One Year to a Writing Life: Twelve Lessons to Deepen Every Writer's Art and Craft.* New York: Marlowe, 2007.

Weldon, Michele. *Writing to Save Your Life: How to Honor Your Story through Journaling.* Minneapolis: Hazeldon, 2001.

Zinsser, William, ed. *Inventing the Truth: The Art and Craft of Memoir.* New York: Houghton Mifflin, 1998.

——. *On Writing Well.* New York: HarperCollins, 2006.

CONTRIBUTORS

ZAN BOCKES (pronounced "Bacchus") earned an M.F.A. in creative writing from the University of Montana. Her fiction, nonfiction, and poetry have appeared in numerous magazines, including *Poetry Motel, Visions International,* the *Pedestal,* the *Comstock Review, Cutbank,* and *Phantasmagoria.* She has had three nominations for a Pushcart Prize. A current resident of Missoula, Montana, she works as a residential sanitation specialist for her own housekeeping business, Maid in Montana, and shares a funky old house with her husband and two exceptional cats.

JAMES BROWN is the author of *The Los Angeles Diaries: A Memoir.* His work has appeared in *Gentleman's Quarterly,* the *New York Times Magazine,* the *Los Angeles Times Magazine, Esquire,* and *Best American Sports Writing 2006.* He has received the Nelson Algren Award in short fiction and a National Endowment for the Arts fellowship.

WENDY CALL is coeditor of *Telling True Stories: A Nonfiction Writers' Guide.* She is a recent writer in residence at Seattle University and Richard Hugo House, Seattle's literary center. Her Web site is http://www.wendycall.com.

KAREN DE BALBIAN VERSTER'S work has been published in numerous literary reviews and anthologies. Her first novel, *Boob: A Story of Sex, Cancer & Stupidity,* was published in 2006. She is currently writing her second novel, *A Basket of Kisses.* Her Web site is http://mysite.verizon.net/kdebv.

JOHN DUFRESNE is the author of six books, most recently the novel *Requiem, Mass.* and a book on writing novels, called *Is Life Like This?* His full-length play, *Trailerville,* was produced in New York at the Blue Heron Theater. He is the coauthor of the screenplay, *To Live and Die in Dixie,* a film released in June 2008. His story "The Timing of Unfelt Smiles" was featured in *Best American Mystery Stories 2007.* He teaches creative writing at Florida International University in Miami.

KATHLEEN GERARD'S writing has been widely published, anthologized, and featured on National Public Radio (NPR). Her plays have been staged and performed both regionally and off-Broadway in New York City. Her work was awarded the Perillo Prize, was a finalist for the Eric Hoffer Award, and was nominated for *Best New American Voices.* She is currently at work on a novel.

REGINALD GIBBONS recently edited *Goyen: Autobiographical Essays, Notebooks, Evocations, Interviews,* a posthumous collection of writings of William Goyen (1915–1983), American author of *The House of Breath* and other fiction. Gibbons's 2008 books include a new collection of poems, *Creatures of a Day,* and translations of *Selected Poems of Sophokles.* He is a professor of English and classics at Northwestern University, and he also teaches in the M.F.A. Program for Writers at Warren Wilson College.

SUE GRAFTON entered the mystery field in 1982 with the publication of *"A" Is for Alibi,* which introduced female hard-boiled private investigator Kinsey Millhone, who operates out of the fictional town of Santa Teresa (a.k.a. Santa Barbara) California. *"B" Is for Burglar* followed in 1985, and since then she has added eighteen novels to the series, now referred to as "the alphabet mysteries." *"U" Is for Undertow* has been completed and is slated for publication in December 2009.

ROBIN HEMLEY is the author of eight works of fiction and nonfiction, most recently *Do-Over!* He has published in numerous magazines and anthologies, including the *New York Times, New York Magazine,* the *Chicago Tribune,* the *Wall Street Journal,* the *Far Eastern Economic Review,* and *McSweeney's Internet Tendency.* His work has been widely anthologized in publications such as The Pushcart Prize: Best of the Small Presses series and the *Touchstone Anthology of Creative Nonfiction.* He is the recipient of awards such as a Guggenheim fellowship, the Nelson Algren Award for fiction, and the Independent Press Book Award for nonfiction. He teaches in the Nonfiction Writing Program at the University of Iowa, and he is the founder and coordinator of the biennial NonfictioNow Conference.

DORIANNE LAUX was a finalist for the National Book Critics Circle Award. Her fourth book of poems, *Facts about the Moon,* is the recipient of the Oregon Book Award and was short-listed for the Lenore Marshall Poetry Prize. Laux is also author of *Awake, What We Carry, Smoke,* and *Superman: The Chapbook.* She is coauthor of *The Poet's Companion* and the recipient of two Best American Poetry Prizes, a Best American Erotic Poems Prize, a Pushcart Prize, two fellowships from the National Endowment for the Arts, and a Guggenheim fellowship. Her work has appeared in the *Best of APR, The Norton Anthology of Contemporary Poetry,* and many others. She taught for fifteen years at the University of Oregon in Eugene and since 2004 at Pacific University's Low-Residency M.F.A. Program. She and her husband, poet Joseph Millar, recently moved to Raleigh, where she joined the faculty at North Carolina State University.

PHILLIP LOPATE is the author of more than a dozen books, the most recent, *Two Marriages* (novellas) and *Notes on Sontag.* He is the editor of five anthologies, including *The Art of the Personal Essay.* In addition his work has been collected in a Phillip Lopate reader, *Getting Personal: Selected Writings.* He is the recipient of numerous awards, including two National Endowment for the Arts grants, and is a professor at Columbia University.

REBECCA MCCLANAHAN has published nine books, most recently *Deep Light: New and Selected Poems 1987–2007* and *The Riddle Song and Other Rememberings,* which won the 2005 Glasgow Award for nonfiction. Her work has appeared in *The Best American Essays,* the Pushcart Prize anthology, and The Best American Poetry series. She lives in New York and teaches in the low-residency M.F.A. programs of Queens University (Charlotte) and Pacific Lutheran University (Tacoma).

KYOKO MORI is the author of three nonfiction books, *Yarn: Remembering a Way Home, The Dream of Water: A Memoir,* and *Polite Lies: On Being a Woman Caught between Cultures,* and three novels, *Shizuko's Daughter; One Bird, Stone Field;* and *True Arrow.* Her essay "Yarn" appeared in *The Best American Essays 2003.* Mori grew up in Kobe, Japan, and spent much of her adult life in the American Midwest before moving to the East Coast. She currently teaches in the M.F.A. Program at George Mason University and lives in Washington, D.C.

BONNIE MORRIS is a women's studies professor at George Washington University and Georgetown University, and she is on the board of Mothertongue, D.C.'s spoken-word stage for women. The author of eight books—including two Lambda Literary Award finalists, *Girl Reel* and *Eden Built by Eves*—she has kept a journal since age twelve and is presently on notebook number 150. "Dr. Bon" has contributed essays, articles, and short stories to more than sixty anthologies of women's writing; her most recent book, *Revenge of the Women's Studies Professor,* is based on her one-woman play about homophobia in higher education.

MARK PAWLAK is the author of five poetry collections, most recently *Official Versions.* His poetry and prose have appeared widely in journals and anthologies, including *The Best American Poetry 2006.* He is the editor of four anthologies, and the most recent is *Present/Tense: Poets in the World,* a collection of contemporary American political poetry. He is coeditor/publisher of the Brooklyn-based Hanging Loose Press. He supports his poetry habit by teaching mathematics at the University of Massachusetts, Boston, where he is director of Academic Support Programs. He lives in Cambridge, Massachusetts, with his wife and teenage son.

DIANA M. RAAB is author of six books of nonfiction and poetry, including the award-winning books *Regina's Closet: Finding My Grandmother's Secret Journal* and *Dear Anaïs: My Life in Poems for You.* Her work has been widely published in literary journals and anthologies such as the *Writer, Writers' Journal,* the *Louisville Review,* the *Litchfield Review, Rosebud, Alehouse, Palo Alto Review,* and the *Rambler.* She teaches in the UCLA Extension Writers' Program and facilitates journaling workshops around the country for professional and emerging writers, high-risk students, and cancer survivors. Her Web site is http://www.dianaraab.com.

PETER SELGIN'S first book of stories, *Drowning Lessons,* won the 2008 Flannery O'Connor Award for fiction. His novel, *Life Goes to the Movies,* was a finalist for the James Jones First Novel Fellowship and the Association of Writers and Writing Programs Writing Award. His work has appeared in many magazines and anthologies, including *Salon,* the *Sun, Ploughshares, Glimmer Train, Missouri Review, Writing Fiction,* and *Best American Essays.* He is the author of two books on the craft of writing, *By Cunning & Craft: Sound Advice and Practical Wisdom* *for Fiction Writers* and *Fiction Matters* (forthcoming). He leads an annual writing workshop in Italy and edits *Alimentum: The Literature of Food.*

KIM STAFFORD is the founding director of the Northwest Writing Institute in Oregon and author of a dozen books of poetry and prose, including *The Muses among Us: Eloquent Listening and Other Pleasures of the Writer's Craft* and *Early Morning: Remembering My Father, William Stafford.*

MAUREEN STANTON'S essays and memoirs have appeared in *Fourth Genre, Creative Nonfiction, River Teeth, Crab Orchard Review,* the *Sun,* and other journals and anthologies. Her nonfiction has received the *Iowa Review* Award, the *American Literary Review* Award, and the Thomas J. Hruska Award in nonfiction from the journal *Passages North.* She has received grants from the National Endowment for the Arts and the Maine Arts Commission. She teaches in the Ph.D. program in creative writing at the University of Missouri in Columbia.

ILAN STAVANS is the Lewis-Sebring Professor in Latin American and Latino Culture at Amherst College. His books include *On Borrowed Words, Dictionary Days, The Disappearance,* and *Resurrecting Hebrew.* He edited the three-volume *Isaac Bashevis Singer: Collected Stories* and *The Poetry of Pablo Neruda,* among others.

MICHAEL STEINBERG is the founding editor of the journal *Fourth Genre: Explorations in Nonfiction.* His most recent books include *Peninsula: Essays and Memoirs from Michigan; Still Pitching,* winner of the 2003 *Foreword Magazine* Independent Press Memoir of the Year; and *The Fourth Genre: Contemporary Writers of/on Creative Nonfiction* (fifth edition), coedited with Robert Root. His shorter works have appeared in many literary journals and anthologies. He is currently writer in residence in the Pine Manor College / Solstice Low-Residency M.F.A. Program.

KATHERINE TOWLER is author of the novels *Snow Island* and *Evening Ferry.* The third volume of her New England Trilogy will be published in 2010. She has been awarded fellowships from the New Hampshire State Council on the Arts and Phillips Exeter Academy, where she served as the Bennett Fellow. She teaches in the M.F.A. Program in Writing at Southern New Hampshire University and lives with her husband in Portsmouth, New Hampshire. Her Web site is http:// www.katherinetowler.com.

TONY TRIGILIO'S recent publications include the poetry collection *The Lama's English Lessons* and the chapbook *With the Memory, Which Is Enormous.* He also coedited the anthology *Visions and Divisions: American Immigration Literature, 1870–1930.* He teaches in the Creative Writing-Poetry Program at Columbia College, Chicago, and coedits the poetry magazine *Court Green.*

LORI VAN PELT wrote *Amelia Earhart: The Sky's No Limit,* which made the New York Public Library's "Best Books for the Teen Age 2006" list. The title story in her short fiction collection, *Pecker's Revenge and Other Stories from the Frontier's Edge,* won the 2006 Western Writers of America Spur Award for best short fiction. She is also the author of the nonfiction Wyoming-based Dreamers and Schemers series published by High Plains Press. She lives with her husband on their cattle ranch near Saratoga, Wyoming. Her Web site is http://www.lorivanpelt.com.

MICHELLE WILDGEN is the author of the novels *But Not for Long* and *You're Not You* and the editor of the anthology *Food & Booze: A Tin House Literary Feast.* Her work has appeared in the *New York Times, O,* the *Oprah Magazine, Best Food Writing, Best New American Voices,* and several journals and anthologies. She is a senior editor at *Tin House Magazine.*

KATHRYN WILKENS'S writing has appeared in the *Los Angeles Times, Writers' Journal, America West Magazine, ByLine, Verbatim,* the *Christian Science Monitor, Writer's Forum, Romantic Homes, Futures* and three anthologies—*Gardening at a Deeper Level, The Walker Within,* and *Chicken Soup for the Soul: My Resolution.* She is a member of the American Society of Journalists and Authors.